THE REAL COWBOYS & ALIENS
OLD WEST UFOS
1865-1895

By Noe Torres & John LeMay

ROSWELL BOOKS.COM
Roswell, New Mexico · Edinburg, Texas

© COPYRIGHT 2020 Noe Torres & John LeMay
All rights reserved.

Cover Illustration by Jolyon Yates

Torres, Noe.
LeMay, John.
 The Real Cowboys and Aliens:
 Old West UFOs (1865-1895)
  1. History—Old West. 2. Ufology—Study of
     Unidentified Flying Objects. 3. Folklore, Old
     West.

A Flying Machine

Between 6 and 7 o'clock last evening while C.A. Youngman and Ben Floxner were standing at a side window of Haddart's drugstore, at Second and Chestnut streets, looking, they discovered an object high up in the air apparently immediately above the Ohio River Bridge, which they at first thought was the wreck of a toy balloon. As it got nearer they observed that it had the appearance of a man surrounded by machinery, which he seemed to be working with his feet and hands. He worked his feet as though he was running a treadle and his arms seem to be swinging to and fro above his head, though the latter movement sometimes appeared to be executed with wings or fans. The gazers became considerably worked up by the apparition, and inspected it very closely. They could see the delicate outlines of machinery, but the object was too high up to make out its exact construction. At times it would seem to be descending, and then the man appeared to exert himself considerably, and ran the machine faster, when it would ascend again and assume a horizontal position. It did not travel as fast as a paper balloon, and its course seem to be entirely under the control of the aeronaut. At first it was traveling in a southeastward direction, but when it reached a point just over the city, it turned and went due south, until it had passed nearly over the city, when it taxed to the southwest, in which direction it was going when it passed out of sight in the twilight of the evening. The gentleman who saw it are confident that it was a man navigating the air on a flying machine. His movements were regular, and the machine was under the most perfect control. If he belongs to this mundane sphere he should have dropped his card as he passed over, to enlighten those who saw him, and that his friends, if he has any, might be informed of his whereabouts.

Example of Ball Lightning c.1901.

Noe Torres: For my wife Robin and son Stephen, with whom I have spent long hours gazing up into the night sky, pondering the wonders of the universe and feeling the immensity of our confinement upon this "pebble in the sky."

John LeMay: For my friends Dennis and Debbie Balthaser, two of the nicest folks in Roswell!

ACKNOWLEDGMENTS

This book, and the others in this series, would never have been written without the encouragement and support of a long list of dear friends, not the least of which is Ruben J. Uriarte, fellow traveler on our amazing interstellar flight.

PREFACE

ACCORDING TO most historians, the period officially designated as the "Wild West" began after the end of the Civil War, lasting from 1865 to 1895. That first year was a wild one, too. It saw the Battle of Palmito Ranch in Brownsville, Texas on May 13th, marking the final armed conflict of the Civil War. It also saw "Wild Bill" Hickok kill gambler Davis Tutt in Springfield, Missouri. It was the quintessential one-on-one duel to later be popularized in movies and television westerns. The event made Hickok a household name. The next year, in 1866, Frank and Jesse James robbed their first bank, while in the Spring, the great cattle drives began in Texas.

Another momentous occasion was upon us in May of 1869. On the 10th of that month, Leland Stanford drove the Golden Spike that joined the rails of the Central Pacific and Union Pacific railroads at a special ceremony in Utah Territory. This completed the First Transcontinental Railroad. Though not recorded in the history books, five days later, something possibly even more momentous happened: a UFO landed in Virginia City, Nevada. Another landed in Pennsylvania that same year.

You see, these are the things the history books neglect to tell you about the Old West. Just like today, strange things were seen in the skies back then. In fact, some of the most famous places and events in Western history have surprising ties to UFOs and their mysterious occupants.

Among the more famous Wild West Incidents were the Gunfight at the O.K. Corral in Tombstone, Arizona, and the Lincoln County War in New Mexico. The Lincoln County War was a feud between political parties that fought over land and cattle. In the middle of it all was a young desperado known as Billy the Kid. Billy was employed by legendary John Chisum, who was fighting it out with Lawrence G. Murphy in Lincoln. In the end, neither side truly won the war and Billy got the shortest end of the stick.

When John Chisum didn't pay Billy his wages after the conflict had ended, Billy took to rustling Chisum's cattle. Chisum, naturally, didn't like this and had a hand in getting Pat Garrett elected as Sheriff of Lincoln County for the express purpose of having Garrett put a stop to the Kid. As someone who knew Billy, Garrett was the perfect man for the job.

In July of 1881, Garrett tracked Billy to Fort Sumner and shot him dead. With the Kid gone, other cattle rustlers took note and began to ease up on their thieving. That same year the famous O.K. Corral gunfight took place.

Though the most famous gunfight of the Wild West, it was in fact only 30 seconds long! The shootout involved the Earp brothers (Virgil, Morgan and Wyatt) and Doc Holiday fighting it out against a group of outlaws nicknamed the "Cowboys."

After the invention of moving pictures, both the Lincoln County War and the O.K. Corral shootout were immortalized several times over in movies. However, the locales of these two marquee Wild West events have a much stranger, hidden history.

About ten years after the gunfight at the O.K. Corral, two ranchers came riding into Tombstone claiming to have shot a large, winged dinosaur -- a pterodactyl -- out in the desert! The prehistoric monstrosity was certainly a different type of "unidentified flying object" when the men first saw it and shot at it with their Winchesters. Rather than a surviving dinosaur, some people believe the creature flew from the prehistoric ages into an intergalactic portal and into the future of 1890. One such alleged portal, the so-called "Lordsburg Door," is located not too far away in New Mexico. And speaking of New Mexico, would you be surprised to learn that Pat Garrett and John Chisum both lived in Roswell during the Lincoln County War? If you didn't know this, that's probably because the two men's history has become overshadowed by something else where Roswell is concerned, the famous UFO crash of 1947.

In July of 1947, a cowboy named Mack Brazel found strange, unearthly debris scattered across the sheep ranch where he was foreman. He reported his find to the U.S. Army in Roswell, which quickly dispatched soldiers to gather the debris and then instigated a cover-up to hide the fact that an extraterrestrial spaceship had crashed in the New Mexico desert.

Most people today are aware of the famous Roswell Incident, but very few of them realize that forty years earlier, Mack Brazel's cousin, Jesse Wayne Brazel, shot and killed Pat Garrett along a desert road. Yes, as shocking as it may seem, two of New Mexico's greatest historical stories share a familial connection.

Back to the Roswell Incident, would you be even more shocked to learn that wasn't the first UFO crash? As it turns out, the Old West saw several Roswell-like incidents where an unexplained object fell out of the sky, including a number that happened well before the world-famous 1897 Aurora, Texas, UFO crash.

As you read this book, we hope that you will be shocked to learn of this hidden history of the "Wild West" period. One where giant swords fall from the sky, families psychically project themselves onto Mars, aliens emerge from the water rather than the sky, and the Men in Black ride around in a futuristic buggy. So, while the Old West was filled with gunfighters, lawmen and outlaws, in the pages ahead you will learn that so too was it populated with strange flying machines and their even stranger pilots.

CONTENTS

ACKNOWLEDGMENTS vi
PREFACE vii

CHAPTERS

1.	The First Pioneers on Mars	13
2.	A Ball of Fire Lands in Nevada	21
3.	UFO Eclipse	27
4.	UFO Landing in Pennsylvania	35
5.	Early Alien Abductions Near Area 51	41
6.	Men in Black in the Old West	49
7.	Flying Serpents and UFOs	57
8.	The First Pascagoula Incident	65
9.	Flying Coffin from Outer Space	73
10.	Ghost or High Tech Humanoid	81
11.	Astronomer Spots Five UFOs	87
12.	The Farmer and the Flying Saucer	93
13.	Drones in the 19th Century	97
14.	Prospector Abducted by Ghost Ship	103
15.	Shining Sphere of the Sun	111
16.	Phantom Train or UFO	121
17.	The Jupiter UFO	129
18.	Mothership Over New Jersey	135
19.	Mysterious Airship Over Iowa	143
20.	New Mexico's First UFO	151
21.	Aliens on the Bridge	159
22.	Spring-Heeled Jack in Kentucky?	165
23.	Mystery Lights of Marfa, Texas	175
24.	The Sword From Outer Space	185
25.	Cowboys Witness UFO Crash	191
26.	Saturn-shaped, Mile-long UFO	201
27.	UFO Crash in the Missouri River	211
28.	The Sasquatch From Outer Space	215
29.	Connecticut Underwater UFO	221
30.	Alien Artifact Unearthed?	227

31.	They Came From the North Pole	237
32.	Unidentified Prehistoric Object	245
33.	California "Meteor Monsters"	253
34.	UFO Explosion in Texas	261
35.	The Crawfordsville Monster	267
36.	The First Reptilian	277
37.	Alien Submarine or Monster of the Deep?	283
38.	Invasion of the Flying Saucers	291

INDEX 299

ABOUT THE AUTHORS 302

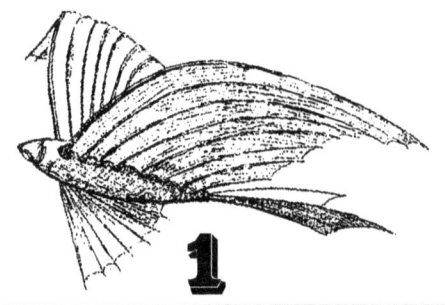

THE FIRST PIONEERS ON MARS

January 12, 1867
Wellesley, Massachusetts

AS AMERICAN ASTRONAUTS of the 21st century explore the surface of the planet Mars, they may want to take some time to look for evidence that people from Earth have visited the planet before – specifically Professor William Denton, a geologist of some note, and his family of Wellesley, Massachusetts. The Dentons claimed to have traveled frequently to Mars and other planets as early as 1867.

An outspoken critic of organized religion, and specifically Christianity, William Denton identified with the beliefs of the Spiritualist movement of the nineteenth century. In addition to believing in the power of the mind and in various supernatural forces, he and his wife Elizabeth were considered radicals for their time in supporting causes such as the elimination of slavery, women's rights, free love, and reforms to capitalism.

Professor William Denton

Over time, the Dentons' studies led them to the idea of "psychometry," a term coined in 1842 by Joseph Rodes Buchanan. Psychometry is the belief that human beings can psychically "link" their minds to an inanimate object, like an ancient weapon or a rock. After linking to it, the information coded into the structure of the object can "transport" a person spiritually to other points where that object has been.

The late Brad Steiger, in his book *Strangers from the Skies*, said this about the Dentons' belief: "A psychometrist is one who 'reads' the history of an object by psychic vibrations which he receives as he holds the thing in his hand. William Denton often said in his lectures that a personal relic of Shakespeare could, in half an hour, reveal more of the bard to one who had the gift of psychometry than biographers have been able to discover in 200 years."

Steiger also quoted Denton as saying, "I have known a little dust from a copper knife to reveal the story of ancient copper-miners of Lake Superior. To the psychometer, the secrets of ancient times are as open as a field in the sunshine. We have only to open our spiritual eyes to discover them!"

Edgar Rice Burroughs Classic A Princess of Mars

Many of the things Denton "saw" during his psychometric experiments were later proven to be accurate. Eventually, he decided to turn this mental power toward the task of transporting himself from the Earth to other planets, chiefly Mars.

Unlike looking at a world through a telescope, Denton believed that "the spiritual faculties enable their possessors to hear, smell, taste, and feel, and become for the time being, almost inhabitants of the planet they are examining."

What he was suggesting is that a person could travel in a virtual or spiritual sense to another planet and experience all the sights and sounds there as if he were physically present on that other world. His idea is uncannily like the theme of Edgar Rice Burroughs' 1911 novel *A Princess of Mars*. Although it is uncertain whether Burroughs ever met or heard of Denton, the protagonist of *A Princess of Mars*, John Carter, transports himself to Mars simply by using the power of his mind.

In 1866, Denton and his son, Sherman, were in their orchard looking up at the planet Venus, when Denton asked his son to visualize what it would be like to be there. Denton later wrote, "I said to Sherman, 'look at that star; and then shut your eyes and tell me what you see.' The boy described strange flora and fauna, including animals that were half fish and half muskrat, and water that was "heavy" but not wet.

Sherman's first visit to Mars came on January 12, 1867, and what he saw is revealed in Denton's book, *The Soul of Things, or, Psychometric Researches and Discoveries, Volume 3*.

OLD WEST UFOS: 1865-1895

Advertisement for Denton's Lectures, circa 1860s

THE REAL COWBOYS & ALIENS

Sherman described monstrous, thorny trees and strange types of fruits and vegetation. He saw creatures that looked like snakes, turtles of varying sizes, frogs, and a creature as large as a horse but nimble enough to jump from tree to tree.

The world around him had lots of bodies of water. He stated, "There is a great deal of water here. From a high place, where I am now, I can see hundreds of lakes."

The American Velocipede, 1868
(Harper's Weekly)

Sherman also met the inhabitants of Mars, who were very much like human beings and were of two genders. Their physical differences were minimal, such as having four fingers and four toes, instead of five. He also noted they had only 16 teeth on the upper jaw and 16 on the lower. Having yellow hair and blue, cat-like eyes, the Martians dressed themselves in a coarse cloth that resembled the clothing of Native Americans. The men wore reddish pants and blue jackets.

In later "trips" to Mars, Sherman saw the inhabitants of Mars moving around in personal flying machines that he said resembled "velocipedes" [bicycles] but that were capable of flight. He also saw larger flying machines that could accommodate as many as 30 people.

While visiting Mars, Sherman was asked questions by his father and was also given directions about things to look for in his surroundings. At one point, he asked his son to look for books and for written documents, in order to get an idea of Martian writing. An example of what Sherman saw is given in Denton's book. Interestingly, similar undecipherable writing has been found at the sites of several reported UFO crashes, including the 1947 Roswell UFO crash.

("See if you can find any books.") "Oh, yes! plenty; but I cannot read them. I see signs too, like short-hand writing. Their words are not made of letters. Their signs are gilt. (Draws Fig. 104.) I see

FIG. 104.—Word-signs.

Many more descriptions are given about life on Mars by Sherman and later by Elizabeth Denton, as well as others who were "transported" to Mars by way of psychometry.

THE REAL COWBOYS & ALIENS

It is important to note that, after hearing all the various accounts of the travelers to Mars, William Denton expressed some doubts about whether they had really visited the Red Planet. Perhaps, he mused, they actually travelled to another place and only thought it was Mars?

Brad Steiger concludes his study of the case by adding, "The Dentons made a very comfortable living on the lecture circuit, giving demonstrations of their psychometric prowess and telling about life on other planets."

In the end, the 1867 expeditions to Mars appear to have been only in the imaginations of William Denton and his family. Still, what if one day our astronauts exploring Mars, while walking across its surface, run across something that looks like ... a 19th century bicycle?

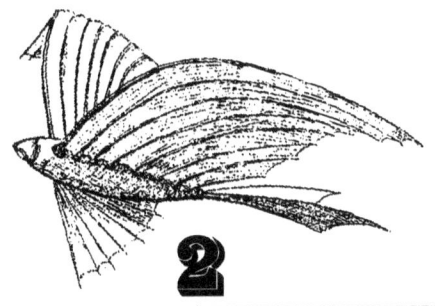

A BALL OF FIRE LANDS IN NEVADA
May 15, 1869
Virginia City, Nevada

ON SATURDAY, MAY 15, 1869, at 2:30 a.m., few people were still awake and walking around town in the small mining community of Virginia City, Nevada, located 25 miles southeast of Reno. In fact, the amazing and highly unusual UFO sighting that was about to happen was probably seen by only two people in the entire town of over 7,000 inhabitants. The incident was witnessed by the narrator of the story, whose name is not given, and a man identified as "Mr. Hayden, doorkeeper of Pike's Opera House."

THE REAL COWBOYS & ALIENS

What the two men saw was so frightening that the narrator of the story later told the local newspaper he thought "that the end of all things was at hand."

Looking off to the western sky, both men noticed a large "ball of fire." The narrator said, "It was immense in size, being apparently about as large as the head of a flour barrel -- larger than the moon when full. It was of a bright glowing red color ..."

Virginia City, Nevada, in 1875

Amazed at the sight above their heads, the narrator said, "...it was sufficiently wonderful to see such an immense ball of fire hanging over the western horizon, even in its quiescent state. It was the strangest sight we ever saw in the heavens...."

But the object, which at first appeared fairly benign, however unusual its appearance, suddenly began to emit strange beams or "rays" of light from all around the circumference of its spherical core. The witness said that "at intervals of a few minutes, [there] darted forth on every side bright rays like the straws of a broom, and from the ends of these were sent out sparks like those from a Roman candle."

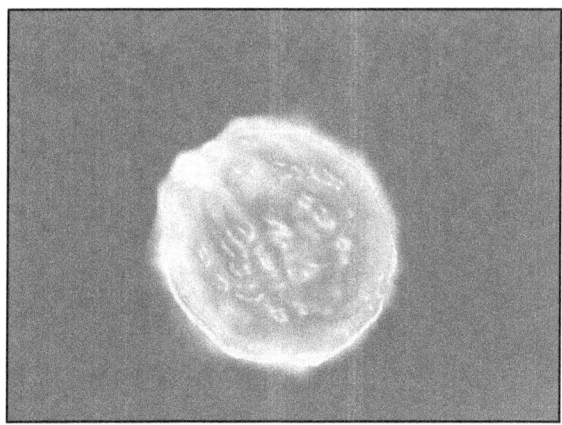
Illustration of Fire Ball

After a few minutes of spewing forth these bright rays of light and sparks, the object would again become simply a ball of fire, before once more emitting the strange rays of light more from its central ball-like structure outward in all directions.

"Its intermittent action and the vehemence with which the rays and sparks were darted forth was the most wonderful part of the phenomenon," said the narrator.

The two witnesses stood aghast as they watched this incredible sight for approximately thirty minutes. At one point, they tried to find others to witness the sight but could locate nobody who was still awake in their immediate area. "Few persons were abroad at the time, and we have been unable to find a gentleman beside the gentleman named, who saw it," said the narrator.

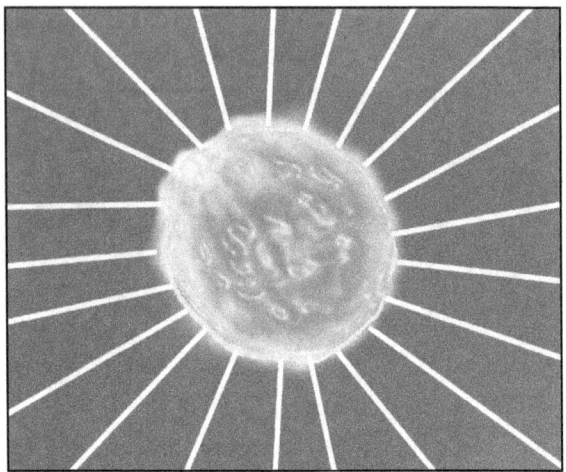

Fireball Emits Rays of Light in All Directions

The witnesses noted that the object, which had appeared in the west, started to move toward a nearby mountain called Mount Davidson, still "blazing and sputtering forth sparks and jets of fire." After they watched it for half an hour, the blazing fireball seemed to slowly settle behind Mount Davidson until it was out of view to the observers.

The object's movement was slow and steady, not unusually fast or slow, according to the witnesses. "It appeared to move with the rest of the heavenly bodies—no faster or slower and went down behind the mountain as steadily as would have been the case with the moon itself."

As far as the distance from the observers to the object, it was difficult to tell, said the witnesses. "It was impossible to judge as to the distance of the meteor. It appeared near enough to have been in the atmosphere of the Earth, indeed appeared to be but a few miles away, yet it may have been a world on fire millions of miles away."

Period Illustration of Virginia City, Nevada

"It was the strangest sight we ever saw in the heavens, and we would have cheerfully bet ten cents that the end of all things was at hand."

"What it was God only knows but we are inclined to think it was a star being consumed and shall not be surprised to hear that one of considerable magnitude is missing."

This amazing UFO sighting was reported in the *Virginia City (Nevada) Territorial Enterprise* for May 16, 1869, the *San Francisco (California) Examiner* on May 21, 1869, and in the *Fort Wayne (Indiana) Daily Democrat* for June 9, 1869. The original *San Francisco Examiner* article follows:

Strange Phenomenon in the Heavens.

Yesterday morning, about half-past two o'clock, a meteor or ball of fire made its appearance in the western sky, and remained visible for at least half an hour. It was immense in size, being apparently about as large as the head of a flour barrel—larger than the moon when full. It was of a bright, glowing red color, and, at intervals of a few minutes, darted forth from every side bright rays like the straws of a broom, and from the ends of these were sent out sparks like those from a Roman candle. Suddenly this would cease, and only the circle or ball of fire remained, when again the rays would blaze out around the whole circumference of the central ball.

In company with Mr. Hayton, doorkeeper of Piper's Opera House, we watched this strange meteor for at least half an hour, when it went down behind Mount Davidson, still blazing and sputtering forth sparks and jets of fire. It appeared to move with the rest of the heavenly bodies—no faster or slower, and went down behind the mountain as steadily as would have been the case with the moon itself. It was impossible to judge as to the distance of the meteor. It appeared near enough to have been in the atmosphere of the earth, indeed appeared to be but a few miles away, yet it may have been a world on fire millions of miles away. Its intermittent action and the vehemence with which the rays and sparks were darted forth was the most wonderful part of the phenomenon—though it was sufficiently wonderful to see such an immense ball of fire hanging over the western horizon, even in its quiescent state. It was the strangest sight we ever saw in the heavens, and we would have cheerfully bet ten cents that the end of all things was at hand. Few persons were abroad at the time, and we have been unable to find a man besides the gentleman named who saw it. What it was, God only knows, but we are inclined to think it was a star being consumed, and shall not be surprised to hear that one of considerable magnitude is missing.—[Territorial Enterprise, May 16th.

San Francisco Examiner, 5-21-1869, p. 1

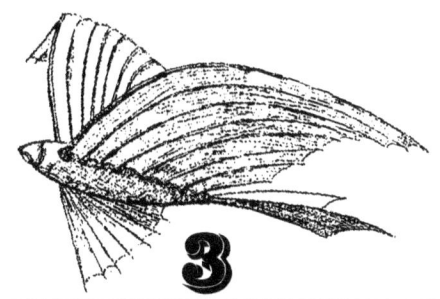

3

UFO ECLIPSE
August 7, 1869
North America

ON AUGUST 21, 2017, the whole of North America, from coast to coast, was treated to the amazing spectacle of a total solar eclipse. It was the first such eclipse seen by the entire nation since 1918, and Americans went outside in droves to witness the rare event. Along with the large numbers of outdoor spectators, the eclipse also brought with it a dramatic increase in UFO sightings, a fact not widely reported by the news media.

During and after the 2017 solar eclipse, the web site of the Mutual UFO Network (MUFON) was inundated by reports from persons who claimed to have seen and, in many cases, photographed one or more UFOs.

Part of the reason for more sightings during an eclipse is simply the fact that more people are observing the sky for longer periods of time, and they are concentrating more fully on what they see up there. They also have cameras, binoculars, and telescopes readily available in preparation for the eclipse viewing. By contrast, on a normal day, the average person pays little attention to the sky and rarely looks up, unless something out of the ordinary happens to draw their attention to it.

Another key is that during an eclipse, the world's top astronomers also have their full attention directed upon on the event. Whereas normally, astronomers might be focused on objects much farther away in the cosmos, during an eclipse, they, to some extent, have their sights, at least temporarily, brought back down to Earth, so to speak.

And perhaps the most important factor about UFO sightings during solar eclipses is that the eclipse itself, especially during totality [the moment when the sun's disc is totally obscured by the moon], seems to bring into view objects, especially near the sun, that would not otherwise be easily visible. This is exactly what happened in the summer of 1869 during a North American total solar eclipse event that we will examine at length in this chapter. The eclipse went as expected, but what was not expected was the discovery by astronomers of a number of mysterious, unidentified objects seen around the sun at about the time of totality.

On August 7, 1869, scientists from around the world gathered at several key locations in North America to witness the solar eclipse, photograph it, and take readings with their various instruments. As was the case in 2017, as well as in other eclipse years, the 1869 event drew a tremendous amount of attention among not just the scientific community but the general public as well.

Joseph Zentmayer

Some of America's top astronomers gathered at three different sites in Iowa to study the event, as well as in Alaska, Virginia, Dakota Territory, Illinois, and Kentucky.

At the Ottumwa, Iowa observation station, one of the scientists gathered for the event, Professor Joseph Zentmayer, noticed something very peculiar about 25 minutes prior to the totality of the solar eclipse.

Zentmayer observed several bright objects crossing from one cusp to the other of the solar crescent. Each object took two seconds to make the crossing. The points were well-defined and must have been miles away from the telescope, given their sharpness.

THE REAL COWBOYS & ALIENS

At the observation point in Shelbyville, Kentucky, astronomer Alvan Graham Clark stated that his attention was called by astronomer Joseph Winlock to small objects crossing the field of the view finder, in straight lines, and supposed by both observers to be meteors. Clark himself observed about twenty of these objects.

Alvan Graham Clark

Also, in Shelbyville, George W. Dean of the U.S. Coast Survey observed, "Soon after the re-appearance of the Sun, my attention was attracted to bright points of light, which were, from time to time, passing across the field. After observing about fifteen or twenty, I concluded that they passed between the Earth and the dark body of the Moon; that they always fell in the same direction, which was from the apparent upper limb of the Moon to the horizon; that their paths were straight lines and parallel to each other; that one seen by Alvan G. Clark, Jr., through a telescope was also seen by myself; and that they were incandescent bodies. In size they were equal to the smallest star visible through any telescope; about as large as a tenth or eleventh magnitude star appears to be in the Harvard College equatorial, [14.9 inches]. As the sunlight increased these meteors ceased to be visible."

Was It a Fleet of UFOs Moving Across the Moon During the Eclipse? (Illustration by Authors)

Dean also later stated, "About ten minutes after the total phase, I observed a faint object pass across the Moon in a southwesterly direction; in a few minutes, I saw another which was soon followed by another in the same general direction. Within fifteen minutes, I saw ten of these faint objects pass across the Moon. They had the appearance of being meteors, and I am inclined to believe they were."

In Falmouth, Kentucky, during totality, an observer identified as Mrs. Murphy saw two "meteors." The first was traced from a point near the meridian and not far from the zenith towards the southeast; the course of the second was from the northwestern to the southwestern part of the sky.

Other sightings of similar objects were reported by Professor Lewis A. Swift in Mattoon, Illinois. Swift was an acclaimed astronomer and renowned comet hunter who discovered 13 comets in his lifetime.

Lewis A. Swift

The fact that several observers in different locations saw the same thing tends to confirm the objects as having been real. They were definitely not, as some skeptics suggested, local insects or seeds picked up by the wind and blown in front of the telescopes. All of the astronomers felt they were something unusual and out of the ordinary.

OLD WEST UFOS: 1865-1895

Were they truly meteors, as most of the men suggested, or where they something entirely different? UFO researchers who have studied this case have, for many years, believed that what the astronomers actually saw in 1869 was a fleet of unidentified flying objects that happened to be in the vicinity of the sun and moon during the total eclipse.

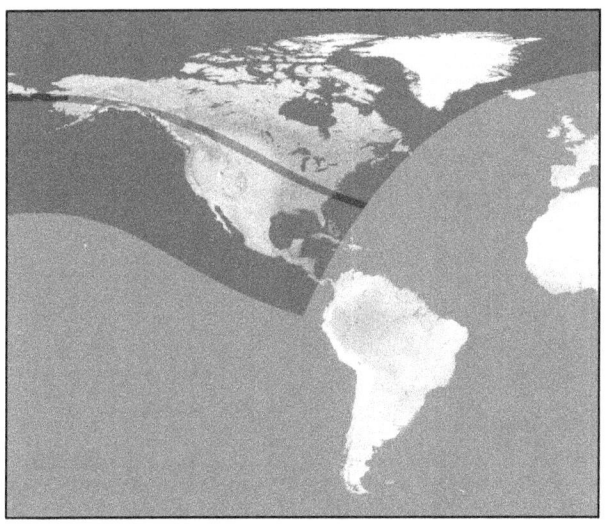

The Path of the 1869 Eclipse
(Courtesy Solar-Eclipse.info)

George W. Dean got the impression that the UFOs had passed "between the Earth and the dark body of the Moon." As many as 20 such objects were spotted, moving in straight lines across the moon. All of which seems to defy the meteor explanation.

In closing, below are the various reports of unusual sightings which were gathered together in the March 1895 edition of *Popular Astronomy* magazine:

> **Meteors Observed During a Total Eclipse of the Sun.**—In looking over the Coast & Geodetic Survey records covering the observations of 1869 during the total solar eclipse, I incidentally gathered the following memoranda of meteors visible by different parties and at different localities. Superintendent's annual report for 1869.
>
> I. *Meteors seen in the Telescope before Totality.*—August 7, 1869, Shelleyville, Kentucky. When the eclipse had advanced half way from the first contact to totality, Alvan G. Clark, Jr., says: "His attention was called, by Professor Winlock, to small objects crossing the field of the finder, in straight lines, and supposed by both observers to be meteors. Mr. Clark himself observed about twenty of these objects." p. 136.
>
> II. *Meteors seen with the unassisted eye during Totality.*—Falmouth, Kentucky, $6^h 15^m$ P. M. "During totality Mrs. Murphy saw two meteors. The first was traced from a point near the meridian and not far from the zenith towards the southeast; the course of the second was from the northwestern to the southwestern part of the sky." p. 132.
>
> III. *Meteors seen in the Telescope soon after Totality.*—Shelleyville, Kentucky, J. Blake, Jr., Alvan G. Clark. "Soon after the re-appearance of the Sun my attention was attracted to bright points of light, which were, from time to time, passing across the field. After observing about fifteen or twenty of them,
>
> *General Notes.* 333
>
> I concluded that they passed between the Earth and the dark body of the Moon; that they always fell in the same direction, which was from the apparent upper limb of the Moon to the horizon; that their paths were straight lines, and parallel to each other; that one seen by Alvan G. Clark, Jr., through a telescope * * * was also seen by myself; and that they were incandescent bodies. In size they were equal to the smallest star visible through any telescope: about as large as a tenth or eleventh magnitude star appears to be in the Harvard College equatorial, [14.9 inches]. As the sunlight increased these meteors ceased to be visible." p. 143.
>
> He was not looking through the telescope during the total phase.
>
> IV. *Meteors seen in the Telescope ten to twenty-five minutes after Totality.*—Shelleyville, Kentucky, George W. Dean. "About ten minutes after the total phase I observed a faint object pass across the Moon in a southwesterly direction; in a few minutes I saw another which was soon followed by another in the same general direction. Within fifteen minutes I saw ten of these faint objects pass across the Moon. They had the appearance of being meteors, and I am inclined to believe they were."
>
> G. D.
>
> # Popular Astronomy.
>
> Vol. II. No. 7.   MARCH, 1895.   Whole No. 17.
>
> **THE STUDY OF PHYSICAL ASTRONOMY—ITS PLACE IN OUR UNIVERSITIES AND COLLEGES**
>
> T. J. J. SEE.

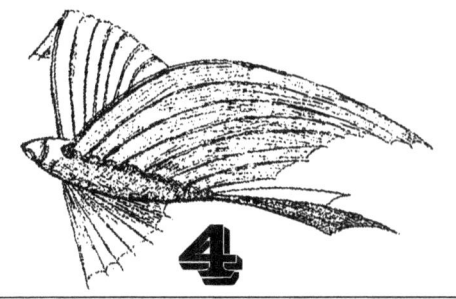

4
UFO LANDING IN PENNSYLVANIA

August 7, 1869
Adamstown, Pennsylvania

AT NOON on Saturday, August 7, 1869, a strange, luminous object came down out of the sky and landed in an empty lot about 200 yards north of the nearby village of Adamstown, Pennsylvania. Today, Adamstown is a borough in Lancaster County, extending into Berks County, in Pennsylvania. The population in 1860 was 462 people.

The controlled landing of the extremely strange object was observed by "four or five different parties" who witnessed from several different vantage points as the bizarre craft settled slowly near the center of the vacant lot.

The landed ship was square near the bottom, and from the square there arose a column of about three to four feet in height and about two feet in thickness. Its surface was like "burnished silver," which shone brightly in the noonday sun. Specifically, the observer said, "The object glittered like a column of burnished silver."

The bright light from the object was almost blinding to the surrounding witnesses. "It seemed to inspire terror rather than admiration," said the reporter who later filed the story for local newspapers. Then, as the witnesses watched in stunned silence, the brightness of the object seemed to gradually fade away.

After about ten minutes, the light had completely faded, and the object that had generated that light was simply no longer there. It had mysteriously vanished.

"After it disappeared, a number of persons visited the spot, but not a trace of anything unusual could be seen."

The newspaper article about this amazing encounter ends by saying, "Similar objects have been seen in the neighborhood on several occasions during the nighttime, but none before in the daytime, or so bright as this."

"The land in the immediate vicinity is dry, there being no swamp about, otherwise the phenomenon might be accounted for [presumably as swamp gas]."

The observed object, due to its small size and odd shape, seems to be almost like a probe or an unmanned drone of some type. The description sounds amazingly like NASA's Mars Explorer probe except for the lack of wheels in this case. Since there were no such things as probes and drones in 1869, its origin would have to be considered unknown. The craft landed in plain view, then became bathed in a bright light, after which it simply was no longer there.

Could It Have Been a Probe to Earth from Another World? Shown is NASA's Mars Explorer Probe

How was the object's disappearance accomplished, one is left to wonder? While the observers were blinded by the bright light, did it take off again and vanish back into the sky? Or, did it somehow transition into another state of matter or another dimension? A third possibility is that the object "cloaked" itself, activating a field of invisibility, after which it may have departed unseen. Yet another theory is that the craft exploded or dissolved, either deliberately (self-destruct) or accidentally.

THE REAL COWBOYS & ALIENS

If the object self-destructed on purpose, perhaps this was necessitated by it having landing in the midst of several eyewitnesses who would no doubt soon approach the ship and endeavor to learn its secrets. The newspaper article states that similar objects had been seen in the same area previously, but all the others had arrived under the cloak of nighttime. The arrival of the August 14 object during the middle of the day may have been a mistake that resulted in its controllers having to self-destruct it.

"The Will o' the Wisp and the Snake" by Hermann Hendrich

The article concludes, "We do not know whether the Jack o' Lantern assumes such large proportions or whether it appears in midday under a bright sun. Perhaps some of our friends versed in the sciences can solve the mystery." The Jack o' Lantern referenced here is not the Halloween variety made with a pumpkin; rather, the term Jack o' Lantern was originally used to describe the visual phenomenon *ignis fatuus* ("foolish fire") known as a *will-o'-the-wisp* in English folklore. This was a phenomenon causing atmospheric "ghost lights" often seen at night, especially over bogs, swamps or marshes. Some believe these strange lights are the result of swamp gas, which has also been used to explain some UFO sightings in more recent times. However, the will-o'-the-wisp or Jack o' Lantern phenomenon is not typically seen in bright daylight and away from swamps.

This UFO landing case from 1869 is one of the most fascinating sightings of the nineteenth century and one that is totally unlike most of the others reported during this time period. The article about it appeared in the August 10, 1869 edition of *The Daily Evening Express* of Lancaster, Pennsylvania, and in the August 16 issue of the *Reading (Pennsylvania) Times*. It has since been featured in many books and other publications dealing with very early UFO sightings. And, like many other cases listed in this book, it remains an enigma to this day.

SINGULAR PHENOMENON.—A most singular phenomenon occurred at midday on Saturday last near the village of Addamstown, Lancaster county. About two hundred yards north of the village is an open lot, and at 12 o'clock, while the villagers were taking dinner, a luminous body was seen to settle near the centre of this lot. It is represented by four or five different parties, who witnessed it from several points, to have assumed a square shape, and shooting up into a column about three or four feet in height and about two feet in thickness. The sun was shining brightly at the time, and under its rays the object glittered like a column of burnished silver. The presence, after reaching its full effulgence, gradually faded away, and in ten minutes time it had entirely disappeared. Those who saw it could not tell what it was. It seemed to inspire terror rather than admiration. After it had disappeared a number of persons visited the spot, but not a trace of anything unusual could be seen. Similar objects have been seen in the neighborhood on several occasions during the night time, but none before in the day time, or so bright as this. The land in the immediate vicinity is dry, there being no swamp about, otherwise the phenomenon might be accounted for.

The Daily Evening Express (Lancaster, PA)
8-10-1869, p. 2

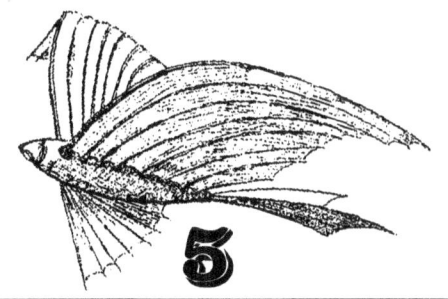

5
EARLY ALIEN ABDUCTIONS NEAR AREA 51

January 16, 1870
Pyramid Lake, Nevada

85 YEARS BEFORE America's top-secret military base known as Area 51 was established at nearby Groom Lake, local Native Americans told stories of strange "little beings" with large heads that abducted humans and took them away, never to be seen again. These strange abductions happened at Pyramid Lake, about 250 miles northwest of the Nellis Air Force Range. The Nellis Range is part of a huge federal compound at the center of which is the mysterious base known as Area 51 located at Groom Lake. It was established in 1955, and the U.S. government has supposedly stored recovered UFOs to study them and attempt to replicate their technology there.

THE REAL COWBOYS & ALIENS

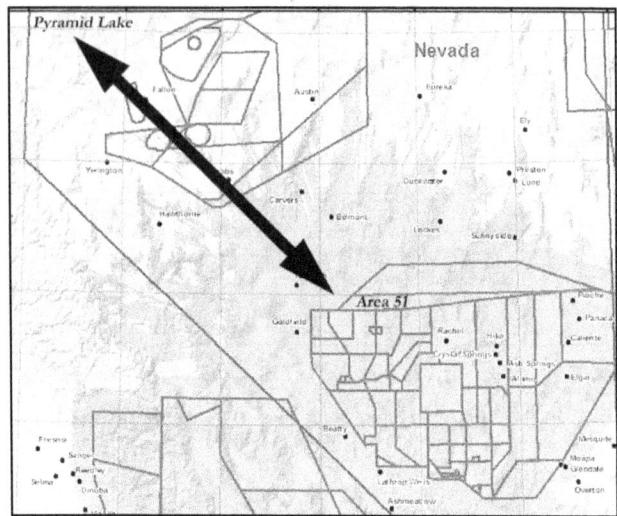

U.S. Air Force Map of Nevada Showing Pyramid Lake relative to Area 51 (USAF)

While it may seem a bit of a stretch to associate Pyramid Lake with Area 51, in truth, it is close enough to make UFO enthusiasts wonder if what happened in 1870 may be linked to the later events associated with Groom Lake. Other than New Mexico, Nevada is arguably the U.S. state most associated with UFOs, due to the presence in the state of Area 51, which the U.S. government did not even admit existed until 2013.

During the 1800s, due to the western states being so sparsely populated, Nevada had very few UFO sightings reported by white settlers, compared to the highly populated eastern states. In fact, most of the earliest reports of UFOs and aliens in Nevada came from the Native American population in the area of Pyramid Lake.

OLD WEST UFOS: 1865-1895

*Native American Cattle Herd near
Pyramid Lake Reservation
Circa 1940 (Library of Congress)*

The lake is a remnant of the great Lake Lahontan of the Pleistocene Era. At that time Lake Lahontan covered most of northwestern Nevada. Today it is located in southeastern Washoe County within the Truckee River Basin and is about 40 miles from Reno. The lake, 356 feet deep at certain points, is named Pyramid Lake due to several pyramid-like formations (called tufa formations) that jut out of the water and line the shores. The largest and best known of these tufa formations is Anaho Island. Though it looks like some ruin of a long-abandoned civilization, it is simply a perfectly natural -- albeit spooky -- formation.

Pyramid Lake was the home to three different but related groups of Native Americans: the

THE REAL COWBOYS & ALIENS

Northern Paiute, the Owens Valley Paiute, and the Southern Paiute. The lake was discovered by white settlers in 1844, having been first spotted by John C. Frémont who gave the lake its name. From this point forward, white settlers began to pour into the area, disrupting the Paiute's way of life. Apparently, the Paiute were not the lake's only residents, however, according to stories told by the natives.

The Paiute spoke of two races of beings that dwelt under the waters of Pyramid Lake. The first was a race of mermaid beings ["merbeings"], and the second was a group of small, child-like creatures they called "Water Babies." But don't let the name fool you, because these "babies" terrified the natives, and for a very good reason, as the strange beings were notorious for abducting humans and dragging them under the lake's surface.

*Charles Kingley's illustration from
The Water Babies.*

OLD WEST UFOS: 1865-1895

Pyramid Lake, Nevada
Copyright by Andrew, Released under CC BY-ND 2.0 (https://creativecommons.org/licenses/by-nd/2.0/)

The image of small, child-like beings with abnormally large heads that appear suddenly and abduct humans falls right in line with more modern stories of alien abductions. Since many UFOs have been spotted in bodies of water, it seems possible that Pyramid Lake in 1870 was being used as a base of operations by these mysterious beings. Their proximity to local human settlements was a bonus that allowed them to quickly obtain laboratory specimens for their otherworldly experiments.

Some researchers have even suggested that, regardless of their origin, these UFO occupants typically establish bases on our planet both deep underground and under our oceans, seas, and lakes.

In ancient fairy lore, beings like these "water babies" appeared often. Students of these fairy legends, which are often eerily similar to UFO stories, theorize that the water babies appeared in the guise of children as a way of enticing human children towards the water, so that the beings might abduct them and drag them to their underwater lair. Like many E.T. encounters, the water babies were said to surface at night and roam the shores, searching for children that had become separated from their parents.

Although Native Americans often had belief systems centered around visitors from outer space, to our knowledge, the Paiute never associated the water babies with these "star people," which does not remove the possibility that they were one and the same. The Paiute, who sometimes threw deformed babies into the lake, believed the water babies were the drowned young come back to haunt them. But still, the description of these strange beings and their habit of abducting humans does seem to line up with other alien abduction narratives.

It is unknown just when the "Water Babies" became known to the white man, but the first to mention them may have been Indian agent Le Bass. The book *The Desert Lake, the Story of Nevada's Pyramid Lake* by Sessions S. Wheeler reproduces a letter from Bass to his superior, the Acting Commissioner of the Office of Indian Affairs, on page 86. The letter, written on January 16, 1870, relates the strange rumors Bass had heard about Paiute superstitions. Bass wrote, "The Indians had superstitious ideas about Pyramid Island. They say that their great grandfathers and grandmothers told them about seeing small

OLD WEST UFOS: 1865-1895

'Indians' that would appear to them at night. Their description of them was a large head and body and short legs, small feet. They believe this but none of them have ever seen it..."

There seems to be an obvious link here between these small beings and the so-called "grey aliens," due to the abnormally large heads in proportion to their bodies. Actually, comparing a grey alien to a human baby isn't terribly far off. However, these frightening "water babies" also displayed behavior not unlike a reptilian in some stories. By "reptilian," we mean the malevolent alien race rumored to exist by many UFO believers. These aliens are said to be shape shifters that can take on human form, though their true physical appearance is closer to that of a scaly reptile in humanoid form.

Take this Paiute story as an example, which is in fact considered to be the origin story of the so-called water babies. At an unspecified location near the lake, a woman had placed her infant on the ground to go gather wood. A serpent-like creature came upon the baby, swallowed it whole, and took on its appearance. When the mother returned, as the "baby" suckled her breast, it also swallowed the mother!

The fear of the water babies has extended into the 21st century, according to David Weatherly's 2019 book *Silver State Monsters: Cryptids & Legends of Nevada*. The book tells the story of Richard Moreno, a Reno, Nevada, newspaper reporter, who asked one of his co-workers of Paiute descent why she chose to build her home in the nearby settlement of Nixon rather than nearer the beautiful Pyramid Lake. She responded, in all seriousness, that she wouldn't dare live near the lake for fear that the water babies would abduct her children.

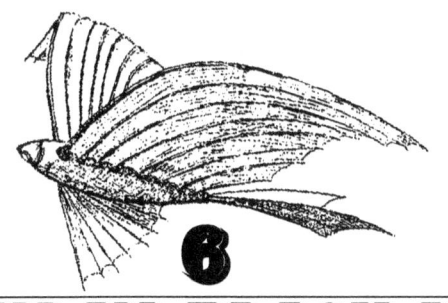

MEN IN BLACK IN THE OLD WEST

March 22, 1873
Taylorsville, Ohio

IN OUR PREVIOUS BOOK, *Early American UFOs*, we examined one of the earliest recorded sightings of the phenomena known as the "Men in Black." Of course, people today know the term thanks to the *Men in Black* motion pictures. In those action-comedy movies, a super-secret organization with high tech weaponry and gadgets protects the Earth from illegal aliens of the extraterrestrial kind. Among the series funnier aspects are the seemingly normal black cars used by the Men in Black that have the ability to go at supersonic speeds and in some cases fly. Oddly, the 1873 newspaper article we will soon discuss is basically a 19th century equivalent of all the elements of the film series -- before any screenwriter could have possibly imagined it!

THE REAL COWBOYS & ALIENS

But first, some history of the real-life Men in Black sightings is in order. The first known instance, that we have thus far been able to discover, of the Men in Black being connected with UFOs happened in June of 1947. In fact, it occurred just one day before Kenneth Arnold's landmark sighting of a mysterious aerial craft that became known, for the first time ever, as a "flying saucer."

The Man in Black encounter began as follows. In the skies over Washington State's Maury Island Sound, a strange craft flew over a fishing party comprised of two men, a boy, and a dog. Debris from the UFO fell from the sky killing the dog. The next day, a lone Man in Black arrived at the scene, collected all the debris, and threatened the witnesses never to speak of the incident.

The next recorded Man in Black sighting came in 1952 and had strange, supernatural attributes to it, such as the Men in Black disappearing in a yellow gas that smelled of sulfur. These men also had the ability to levitate objects with their minds and communicate telepathically.

Another famous sighting seemed to suggest that the Men in Black could be androids. On September 11, 1976, Dr. Herbert Hopkins received a phone call from a stranger asking if he could visit with him regarding an alien abduction case Hopkins was investigating. A very short time later, some say only seconds, there was a knock at the door. Hopkins answered to find a man that he described as looking like a mannequin. He said the man had no hair whatsoever, not even eyebrows or eyelashes! What's more -- he said the man spoke in a stilted, mechanical manner.

As a demonstration of his abilities, the Man in Black gave Hopkins a penny. The man then turned the penny blue and it vanished between his fingers. This strange intimidation ploy was the lead up to the man asking Hopkins to destroy his tapes containing a session with the abductee under hypnosis. Hopkins obliged, and revealed that towards the end of their visit, the stranger's speech suddenly began to "falter" as though his batteries were dying.

In the 1800s, these mysterious Men in Black were usually described as being "ghosts." They were never associated with UFOs until a remarkable incident happened in Taylorsville, Ohio, in 1873 that we are now about to disclose. In the fascinating account reported in the April 8, 1873 edition of no less a publication than the *New York Daily Herald*, a man dressed in a black suit was seen exiting a UFO, stepping into a futuristic land vehicle, and speeding away at a "great velocity" before taking flight.

The article, written by a reporter named W. A. Taylor, originated in the *Zanesville (Ohio) Herald*, published on April 5, 1873, and spread around the country to many other newspapers, including the New York papers. It goes as follows: "A most extraordinary phenomenon was observed near the village of Taylorsville, a few miles from this city, about a week ago. Mr. Thomas Inman, whom your reporter can vouch for as a respectable farmer of unquestionable truth and veracity, related the circumstances to the writer, and, with his son, who was also an eye witness, is willing to make oath to the truth of this statement."

Jack the Ripper was often Depicted as a Man Dressed in all Black.

The article reveals the sighting took place "one evening about two weeks ago" which would make the date around March 22nd. The article continues that "while Mr. Inman and his son, a young man, were returning to their home from Taylorsville, they saw a light, which they describe as looking like a 'burning brush pile,' near the zenith, descending rapidly towards the earth, with a loud roaring noise. It struck the ground in the road, a short distance from them." At this point, the story is no different than a typical early meteor sighting. But just wait and see what happens next. "The blazing object flickered and flared for a few moments and then faded into darkness, as a man dressed in a complete suit of black and carrying a lantern emerged from it."

The significance of this sighting is staggering to modern UFO researchers! Here we have, in 1873, a strange, illuminated, aerial craft descending from the sky, making a pinpoint, controlled landing in a remote area of Ohio, and disgorging from its interior, a nattily dressed Man in Black carrying some type of portable, hand-held light source. After the man exited, the landed object "flickered and flared" before fading "into darkness," suggesting that it either mysteriously vanished or became "cloaked," thereby invisible to local observers.

But even more incredible was what Thomas Inman and his son observed next! According to W.A. Taylor, "The man walked a few paces and stepped into a buggy [the common term for a wheeled land vehicle] which had not been observed before, by either Mr. Inman or his son. There was no horse attached to this super-natural vehicle, but no sooner had the man taken his seat than it started to run, noiselessly but with great velocity along the highway and this it continued to do until it reached a deep gully into which it plunged when buggy, man and lantern suddenly disappeared as mysteriously as they came."

THE REAL COWBOYS & ALIENS

Victorian Era Horse-Drawn Carriage.

Nearly 20 years before the first "horseless carriage" was invented in Germany, this bizarre humanoid got out of his flying craft and mounted what sounds like an ultra-modern automobile, capable of traveling at a "great velocity" and without any apparent noise, which is something that even modern automobiles cannot match. Further, the vehicle later plunged into a "deep gully" and disappeared, suggesting that, in addition to traveling on roads, this incredible car could also fly or hover!

This is certainly one of the most bizarre UFO encounters of its time, incorporating three distinct features rivaling any modern UFO sighting: (1) the controlled landing of a manned vehicle, (2) a land vehicle capable of great velocity and possibly flight, and (3) a Man in Black.

OLD WEST UFOS: 1865-1895

In other chapters of this series, we discuss instances where people of the 1800s seemed to have encountered "time travelers" from the future. This 1873 story certainly seems to qualify as a possible encounter with someone from the future, who arrived in some sort of time machine, which subsequently vanished, and who then stepped into a futuristic land vehicle that had been prearranged for him in which to travel. Obviously the term "buggy" was used at the time for any form of wheeled land vehicle, and the witnesses would not have had any other way of describing what they saw, although the article stated that the conveyance was a "super-natural vehicle," erasing any doubt that it looked like a typical horse-drawn buggy of the day. Even the "lantern" that the stranger was holding in his hand was very likely not a lantern at all, but some type of sophisticated electric torch that the witnesses would not have known how to describe, falling back on the familiar term "lantern."

So there you have it, "truth" that's even stranger than the fiction presented in movies. Not only is this likely the first story to link UFOs with the Men in Black, but it also leaves one with the disturbing suspicion that time travel could have possibly been involved, which goes along with the theory that Men in Black may, in fact, be time travelers.

VERY LIKE A WHALE.

ZANESVILLE, Ohio, April 5, 1873.

TO THE EDITOR OF THE HERALD:—

A most extraordinary phenomenon was observed near the village of Taylorsville, a few miles from this city, about a week ago. Mr. Thomas Inman, whom your reporter can vouch for as a respectable farmer of unquestionable truth and veracity, related the circumstances to the writer, and, with his son, who was also an eye witness, is willing to make oath to the truth of this statement.

One evening about two weeks ago, while Mr. Inman and his son, a young man, were returning to their home from Taylorsville, they saw a light, which they describe as looking like a "burning brush pile," near the zenith, descending rapidly towards the earth, with a loud, roaring noise. It struck the ground in the road a short distance from them. The blazing object flickered and flared for a few moments and then faded into darkness, as a man dressed in a complete suit of black and carrying a lantern emerged from it. The man walked a few paces and stepped into a buggy, which had not been observed before by either Mr. Inman or his son. There was no horse attached to this supernatural vehicle, but no sooner had the man taken his seat than it started to run, noiselessly but with great velocity, along the highway, and this it continued to do until it reached a deep gully, into which it plunged, when buggy, man and lantern suddenly disappeared as mysteriously as they came.

This phenomenon is certainly an extraordinary and unexplainable one, and sounds more like the vagary of a crazed brain than anything else. But both Mr. Inman and his son, who are sober men and not given to superstitious notions, agree precisely in their statements, and maintain that they are strictly true. If it was an optical delusion, superinduced by a meteor or "Jack o' lantern," is it not strange that the same fancied appearances could be conjured up in the minds of two men at the same time? Here is a chance for scientists to explain the fantastical optical and other illusions and delusions which follow in the train of, and are suggested by, some strange and unexpected sight or occurrence.

W. A. TAYLOR.

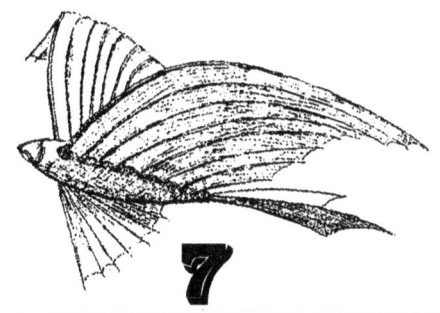

7
FLYING SERPENTS AND UFOS
June 26, 1873
Fort Scott, Kansas

IN THE 1800s, an observer on the ground looking up and seeing an elongated, cylindrical, or cigar-shaped object streaking across the sky would most likely have fallen back on terminology with which they were most familiar, declaring that it was a "flying serpent" or "dragon" or some other form of supernatural manifestation. Such descriptions do not necessarily mean that what was seen in the sky was a biological creature, but rather, that this was the closest analogy that could be drawn by the observer below. Even in modern UFO sightings, aerial craft are sometimes described in biological terms, such as "a giant bird-like object" or "like a whale."

THE REAL COWBOYS & ALIENS

Such is the case with two remarkable UFO sightings that took place in 1873. Researchers over the years have studied these cases closely and concluded that it is very likely that the objects seen were, in truth, metallic aerial craft.

Artist Neil Riebe's Rendering of the "Serpent Encircling the Sun"

At sunrise on June 26, 1873, residents of Fort Scott, Kansas, reported seeing what looked like a "huge serpent" encircling the sun. They saw the object when the sun was about halfway above the horizon. It remained visible "for some moments."

The incident was printed in the local newspaper, the *Fort Scott Monitor*, on the following day, June 27. According to the newspaper, the sighting was reported by two very reliable witnesses. The witnesses were willing to sign sworn statements that

OLD WEST UFOS: 1865-1895

they actually saw the flying serpent. The apparition was reportedly also seen by several soldiers of the U.S. Cavalry, who were stationed in Fort Scott.

> **SINGULAR PHENOMENON.**
>
> **The Sun Encircled by a Serpent.**
>
> A strange and remarkable phenomenon was observed at sunrise yesterday morning. The sky was clear, and the sun rose entirely unobscured. When the disk of the sun was about half way above the horizon, the form of a huge serpent, apparently perfect in form, was plainly seen encircling it, and was visible for some moments. We have this statement from two reliable parties who witnessed the phenomenon, and are willing, if necessary, to make affidavit of their assertions. We have too great respect for the sun to rise before it, and therefore are innocent of the authorship of this "sea serpent" of the sun; but we have all confidence in the credibility of our witnesses. What fearful portent is indicated in this wonderful and ominous phenomenon? We shall join a Sunday school and await the solution.

Original Article from the Fort Scott Monitor

Additionally, a few days earlier, something very similar was seen by a farmer named Mr. Hardin, who lived a few miles east of Bonham, Texas. A serpent-like object appeared in the sky above where Hardin was working. It was also seen by several other workers standing in nearby fields. What they saw was unusual indeed, and the farmers became "seriously frightened," according to the local newspaper.

They described what they saw as an "enormous serpent" that seemed to float upon a cloud. "It seemed to be as large and as long as a telegraph pole, was of a yellow striped color, and seemed to float along without effort," the newspaper reported.

As the farmers continued to watch, the giant snake seemed to drift off toward the east. As it moved along in the sky, the serpent seemed to behave just like a real snake. It would coil itself up, turn over, and thrust its head forward just like a snake when it is about to bite.

The witnesses stated that the flying snake would "thrust forward its huge head as if striking at something, displaying the maneuvers of a genuine snake."

In his 1950 book *The Flying Saucers Are Real*, Donald Keyhoe argued that the sky serpent over Bonham was actually a flying saucer. Keyhoe wrote, "It was broad daylight when a strange, fast moving object appeared in the sky, southwest of the town. For a moment, the people of Bonham stared at the thing, not believing their eyes. The only flying device then known was the drifting balloon. But this thing was tremendous and speeding so fast its outlines were almost a blur."

According to Keyhoe, terrified farmers hid under their wagons and townspeople fled indoors. Only a few people remained outdoors to view the object. The UFO circled the town twice before moving off to the east and disappearing.

The sighting appeared in the *New York Times*, but the story about it poked fun at the witnesses. The New York newspaper said that the farmers who claimed to see the flying serpent must have been delirious.

The *New York Times* also commented about the flying serpent seen in the skies over Fort Scott, Kansas. The writer said that if people continued to see flying snakes, the nation should consider banning the sale of alcoholic drinks.

Some years before these two cases, back in 1857 and 1858, settlers in Nebraska claimed to have also seen a huge flying serpent. Historian Mari Sandoz said that the creature was seen hovering in the sky over a steamboat. The serpent, which appeared to be "wavy," slipped in and out of the clouds. It also seemed to breathe fire and had streaks of light coming out of its sides.

The sighting in Nebraska was later put in a folksong. The song describes the serpent as a "flyin' engine / Without no wing or wheel / It came a-roarin' in the sky / With lights along the side / And scales like a serpent's hide." To some people, this sounds more like an alien craft than a living creature.

Sculpture of the feathered serpent god Quetzalcoatl (Wikimedia)

Flying objects described as "flying serpents" have been seen throughout human history. For example, even the Bible mentions a "fiery flying serpent" (Isaiah 30:6). Paintings and sculptures of flying serpents have been found among artifacts of ancient cultures, such as the Chinese, Maya, and Aztecs. The feathered serpent god Quetzalcoatl was an important part of Aztec religious beliefs.

The June 1873 incidents remain very interesting for a number of reasons. First, the witnesses seem believable. Second, the descriptions of both events were very similar. In all likelihood, what was seen were some kind of advanced flying craft capable of incredible aerial acrobatics.

Of course, skeptics argue that the stories were made up by sensation-seeking newspaper reporters eager to drive up sales of their newspapers. The term for these fake reports is "snaik stories" – the word snake being purposely misspelled to signal a "tall tale." Sometimes stories appeared about winged snakes and other times snakes without wings. However, the 1873 sightings seem to be something entirely different and most likely were real events.

SIGNS AND WONDERS.

A Serpent in the Clouds.

A few days ago a Mr. Hardin, residing some five or six miles east of this place, saw something resembling an enormous serpent floating in a cloud that was passing over his farm. Several parties of men and boys, at work in the fields, observed the same thing, and were seriously frightened. It seemed to be as large and long as a telegraph pole, was of a yellow striped color, and seemed to float along without any effort. They could see it coil itself up, turn over, and thrust forward its huge head as if striking at something, displaying the maneuvers of a genuine snake. The cloud and serpent moved in an easterly direction, and were seen by persons a few miles this side of Honey Grove. The question is, what is it, and where did it come from?—*Bonham (Texas) Enterprise.*

From the Fort Scott Daily Monitor, 6-24-1873, p.4

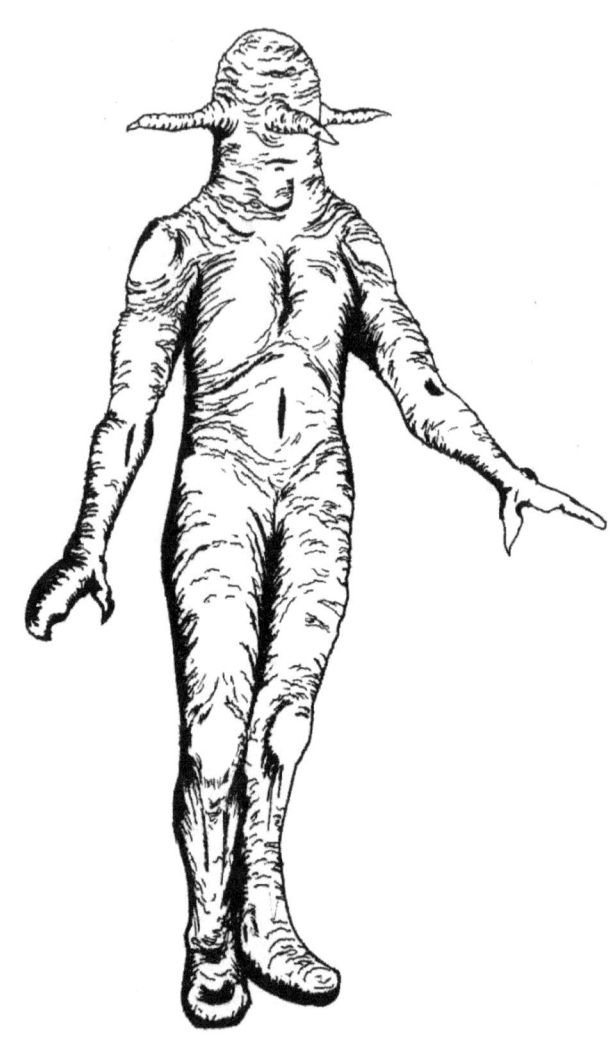

Artist's Rendition of the Bizarre Alien Seen by Parker and Hickson in 1973 (Neil Riebe)

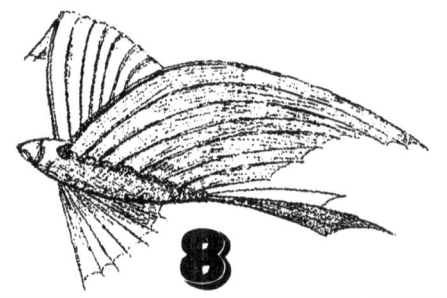

THE FIRST PASCAGOULA INCIDENT

August 13, 1874
Pascagoula, Mississippi

ON THE NIGHT OF August 13, 1874, Pascagoula, Mississippi, was visited by a bizarre unidentified flying object described as a "cloud of light" and also as a "luminous electric cloud." It flew in from the northwest, moved over the western edge of town, and then continued on into the Gulf of Mexico until it was out of view. Although quite an impressive event on its own standing, what is more amazing is what happened nearly 100 years later at one of the points along the flight path of the 1874 UFO. Calvin Parker, who was a consultant for this chapter, and his friend Charles Hickson were fishing along the banks of the Pascagoula River when they saw a large luminous spaceship descend near them. Strange humanoid beings came out of it and took the men into the craft, where the two fishermen underwent some type of bizarre medical exam before being released. Considered one of the most credible and well-documented UFO abduction cases of all time, the October 11, 1973 abduction of Parker and Hickson occurred 99 years after the strange Pascagoula UFO sighting of 1874. Could these two events be somehow related? Is there something about the Pascagoula area that attracts these UFOs? Are the UFO occupants masters of both space and time?

Noe Torres (left) with Pascagoula Abductee Calvin Parker (right) in April 2019

"I'm going to have a banner made that says PASCAGOULA: Gateway to the Stars!" Rebecca Davis, director of Pascagoula Main Street, joked in a 2019 interview for this book. "I do find it odd that it is on the West side just like the Parker-Hickson abduction, and actually Round and Horn Island isn't that far apart." Davis adds that the city of Pascagoula has for many years been steeped in UFO lore, despite the fact that religious conservatives have strongly objected to any discussion of UFOs.

In an article about this case in the *Flying Saucer Review* (v. 35, no. 3, 1990), the editors express their view that the 1874 incident in Pascagoula would have gotten much more media coverage, perhaps even as much as the abduction of Parker and Hickson, if more media outlets had been around in 1874, and if Pascagoula had not been so far off of "the beaten path."

The story of the original incident appeared in the August 22, 1874 edition of *The Chronicle-Star* newspaper of Pascagoula. The article begins, "On the night of the 13th inst., a singular and awe-inspiring phenomenon was observed at the village upon the seashore, corroborated by several reliable witnesses."

Interestingly, the sighting of this strange object occurred during a week of intense heat in Pascagoula. Commenting on the weather during the week of the incident, the local newspaper said, "Hot! Hotter! Hottest! And the hottest weather we have had this week since we have been on the coast, and we learn that the memory of the oldest inhabitant in vain attempts to run back and recollect when it was hotter. Even our previously constant sea breeze at night failed us for a time, and men pantingly sought their porticoes, and out-of-door retreats, endeavoring to obtain sleep. What must it have been up country, away from the coast?"

Just days later, the newspaper reported on the strange phenomenon that flew across town: "The evening had been very close and sultry, and between ten and eleven o'clock, a violent squall and thunderstorm, accompanied with heavy rain and hail came from the north. This did not last more than half an hour, the wind falling and shifting to the west, but coming in fitful gusts, when the luminous electric cloud, for such it seems to have been, passed through the western extremity of the village."

Similar Cloud-like UFO spotted in England in 1965 (Courtesy Flying Saucer Review, v. 12, no. 2, 1966)

"Coming from the northwest, which would be from over the marsh and bays of the Pascagoula rivers, just above their mouths, it moved southeastwardly along the Mound towards Horn

OLD WEST UFOS: 1865-1895

Island past the extreme left flank – so to express it, sweeping over Mrs. Willis's, the White House [a local hotel], and buildings adjacent. It contained intense heat." Calvin Parker, who was abducted in 1973, told the authors that the flight path described in 1874 was right past the site of his encounter, "I know the location he is talking about. If I am right, this happened at almost the same spot where Charlie and I were abducted."

The newspaper account continued, "Mrs. Willis had just put her head out of the front window when she was stifled by the burning hot gust from the west and felt as if her hair had been scorched from her head. She instantly thought 'the house was on fire' and ran back to observe the kitchen. She thinks the heat was sufficient to have set the house on fire had it continued ten minutes. It felt as if she had put her face near a red-hot furnace."

"Mr. Trudel – mine host of the White House – and several of his boarders felt the heat and saw the illuminating cloud. Mr. [Trudel] thought, from the light and heat, that the hotel was on fire, and upon the instant came near sounding the alarm. The heat he imagined had blistered his face and hands and he felt to see if his beard had gone. As it passed, he noticed the light which illuminated the building and surrounding objects."

In *The UFO Book* (p. 572), author Jerome Clark said "It emitted heat so intense that some witnesses thought they or their houses were about to ignite. The object illuminated the ground and buildings underneath it."

THE REAL COWBOYS & ALIENS

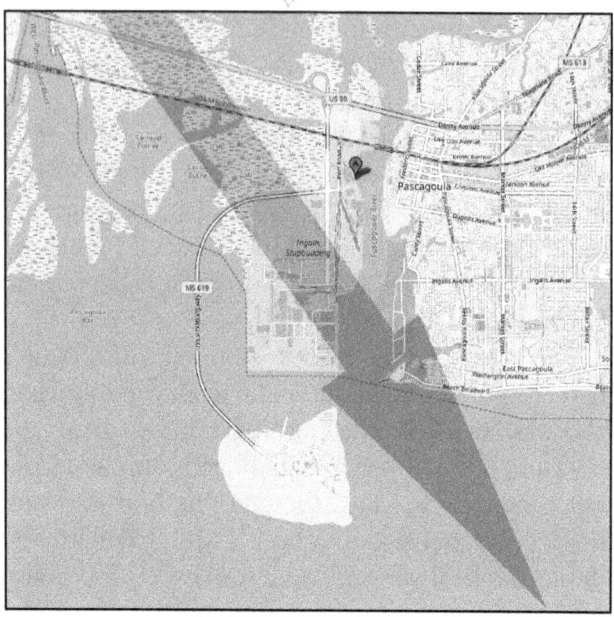

Map Showing Approximate Path of Object and a Marker Placed at Site of 1973 Event

Said the newspaper, "Mr. Ladnier was asleep on the front gallery of the building adjoining the White House, whither he had taken refuge from the rain, was awakened by the intense heat on his face, and clearly observe the cloud of light, moving slowly along and which seemed to be about half a mile long, on a line between him and Round Island, and about thirty feet deep; it illuminated objects that it passed over, and seemed to move about three or four yards above the water, which was of inky blackness below it and all was very dark around, nothing being distinguished except this light. He noticed it pass over a vessel at anchor, about half a mile from shore, when the spars and rigging became distinctly visible. He was much alarmed and remarked to his brother who was with him that 'the world was on fire.'"

"Several others saw and felt this phenomenon. Some thought the 'Comet had struck us,' and others thought 'Judgment day had come.' It soon passed and all was again dark and still."

Interestingly, the community of Winona, located 265 miles to the northwest, also experienced a similar atmospheric phenomenon, except earlier in the day, between 4 and 5 p.m. "Currents of hot air coming in fitful gusts" and feeling "like blasts from a furnace, parching the cheek" were described in the *Winona Advance* newspaper.

Early in 1986, Betty Rodgers, vice-president of the Jackson County Genealogical Society, sent a copy of the 1874 newspaper article to the Climatic Data Center at Asheville, North Carolina, seeking more information about climatic conditions in Pascagoula on the day of the sighting, but they could not find any records. The reply she received stated that the only weather station in Mississippi in 1874 was in Vicksburg, over 200 miles northwest of Pascagoula. However, she was told, it might have been a case of "ball lightning."

Rebecca Davis, director of Pascagoula Main Street, is impressed that Betty Rodgers, a well-respected local historian, made an effort to find out more about the mysterious event. "Ms. Betty knows history, and if she didn't think it was creditable, she would not have sent it to them so maybe there is something there," Davis told us.

THE REAL COWBOYS & ALIENS

Regarding ball lightning, would it realistically remain stable long enough to travel all the way through town? Would it be strong enough to illuminate the entire west side of Pascagoula and generate such an intense heat that witness thought the buildings would catch fire or their facial hair would be burned off? Ball lightning might cause the air to become electrically charged and might create some sparkles of rounded lightning in the sky for short periods of time, typically no more than 10 seconds, but it seems unlikely to produce such extreme effects as were reported in Pascagoula.

The authors did a search of the 1870 and 1880 U.S. Census Bureau data for the surnames mentioned in the original newspaper article - Willis, Trudel, and Ladnier. The name Willis appears in the Pascagoula area, although in the neighboring community of Ocean Springs, located 17 miles away. Quite a number of "Ladniers" are listed as living in Pascagoula on the 1880 census. The name "Trudel" does not appear but could have been misspelled, or the gentleman might have been just passing through.

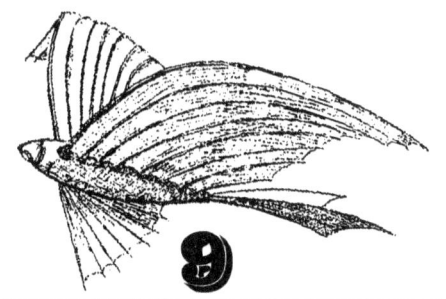

FLYING COFFIN FROM OUTER SPACE

April 10, 1875
Brownsville, Missouri

THERE IS A SUBSET of UFO research that deals with the occasional appearance of mysterious orbs of light that usually hover near the ground and involve groups of relatively small oval balls of light. Although not believed to be aerial craft such as most UFOs are thought to be, these small hovering orbs of light are nonetheless an interesting phenomenon that bears closer study. Sometimes they appear prior or during the sighting of a UFO and could be a kind of drone or unmanned aerial probe. Skeptics try to explain these apparitions away as "ball lightning" or other naturally occurring atmospheric events, but the rest of us aren't quite so certain, especially when a larger UFO is also seen in the area, as in this story from 1875.

THE REAL COWBOYS & ALIENS

1901 Illustration of "Ball Lightning"

Our tale originates in Brownsville, Missouri (now known as Sweet Springs), at the Central Hotel in that town. Sometime around April 10, 1875, a guest of the hotel witnessed something very strange from his window at 11:30 p.m. A newspaper article about the incident began by stating, "Wednesday last was a mild and summer-like day, and old weather prognosticators predicted the coming of good rain. But it is not of the rain we propose to speak, but of the sights that were seen on that night by a number of our citizens."

The article then details how strange lights awakened one of the guests, unfortunately unnamed, who looked out his window. Outside he saw "balls of light from the size of an egg to that of a man's head and changing from a white to that of a reddish glare." The orbs "were floating about in the air, as though they were animate objects."

At first there were only a few, but eventually their number increased to about fifty of them hovering about twenty or thirty feet from the ground. "They moved around like apples on disturbed water, then like they were engaged in a waltz and at times falling into ranks like soldiers marching to and fro," the paper wrote. The balls of light were convening over an old field at the east end of the town. As the witnesses watched the bizarre light show, a cloud suddenly came in from the west "which was about the size of a door, and of a grayish or smoke color."

It is at this point that this somewhat ordinary "mystery orbs" sighting transforms into an actual UFO sighting, with the sudden appearance of a grayish, rectangular UFO shrouded in a cloud. Although the exact size of the UFO is unclear from the description given, it was clearly large enough to elicit wonder and to have it be compared to a "cloud."

The described shape, a "coffin," suggests that the object was like an oblong box, having length, breadth, and depth. Oblong-shaped UFOs more commonly referred to as "rectangular," are quite a common type that have been observed for many years.

The witnesses stated that the strange cloud-like UFO looked like "a black coffin," hovering over the same field where the mysterious orbs of light had appeared. The rectangular UFO came to a stop over the field, hovering about forty or fifty feet above the ground, and the orbs of light began to dance around it in a circular manner until their motion finally came to a halt near the larger object.

*Recent Sighting of Oblong UFOs
(Courtesy Beyond the Strange YouTube Channel)*

What happened next is remarkable. The rectangular UFO opened a hatch or "lid," and all the smaller orbs of light flew inside it, going out of view of the observers. The newspaper account said, "A lid seemed to rise from the coffin, and with slow movements, the lights entered the same, were lost to view. The coffin-like object was then wafted southward...."

Given this description, it becomes even more likely that the smaller orbs of light were drones or probes sent out into the surrounding environment to collect data on the area. Even as humans today use drones to take photos and collect data, these glowing orbs sound like they performed the same functions for whoever the occupants of the rectangular UFO were.

OLD WEST UFOS: 1865-1895

Because the UFO exited the town toward the south, flying over the town's cemetery when it seemed to go out of view, the observers were left with the impression that the UFO had "settled down" into the graveyard, although very likely this was simply their mistaken belief, spurred on by their fear and sense of having experienced something totally unexplained or supernatural. It is far more plausible that the UFO flew over the cemetery and kept right on going.

The newspaper article, published in the *Sedalia (Missouri) Democrat* of April 14, 1875, stated, "The coffin-like object was then wafted southward, and on reaching the graveyard settled down and was seen no more. A great number of our citizens witnessed that night's phenomena which will be very memorable."

Interestingly, the editor of the *Sedalia Democrat* titled the article "Ignis Fatuus," which is Latin for "foolish fire," and is another term for *will o' the wisp*. It is defined as a light that sometimes appears in the night over marshy ground and is sometimes attributable to the combustion of gas from decomposed organic matter. It was an obvious attempt to explain away something that was clearly beyond the normal.

Of note, the Sedalia newspaper gives the original source of the article as the *Brownsville (Missouri) Banner*, dated April 10, 1875. Since the town of Brownsville, Missouri, no longer exists, and all copies of its newspaper appear to have been irretrievably lost, researchers are very thankful that the article was also published by the *Sedalia*

Democrat on April 14. As stated earlier, the town known as Brownsville in 1875 is now called Sweet Springs, Missouri.

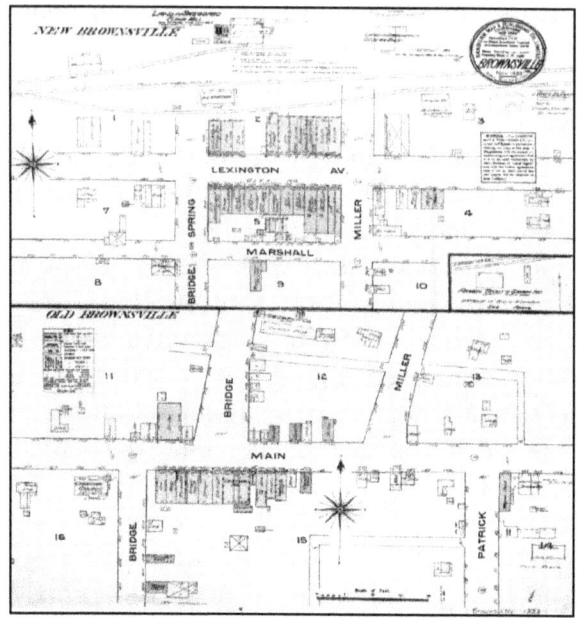

1883 Map of Brownsville, Missouri (Courtesy University of Missouri Digital Library)

This is another of the most truly remarkable UFO sightings of the 19th century, and although the main witness struggled to put what he saw into the words and terminology with which he was familiar, overall we must say that he did a fairly credible job. The end result of his efforts is an amazing tale of close contact with free-floating alien probes that were dispatched to collect data from among the human community of Brownsville, Missouri.

OLD WEST UFOS: 1865-1895

IGNIS FATUUS.

Wednesday last was a mild and summer-like day, and old weather prognosticators predicted the coming of a good rain. But it is not of the rain we propose to speak, but of the sights that were seen on that night by a number of our citizens. About half past eleven or twelve o'clock, an inmate of the Central Hotel, on awakening, had his attention called to a glare of lights which he observed out of his window, near which he was lying. At first he supposed it to be in a dwelling, but there being so many, and at such a late hour, his attention was called to solve what they meant. From the peculiar nature of them, he aroused a number of the inmates to witness the strange proceedings. Balls of light from the size of an egg to that of a man's head, and changing from a white to that of a reddish glare, were floating about in the air, as though they were animate objects. At first there were but few of them, and seemed to be about twenty or thirty feet from the ground, but in a short time the number increased, and a regular carnival was held.

They moved around like apples on disturbed water, then like they were engaged in a waltz, and at times falling into ranks like soldiers, marching to and fro. They appeared to be over an old field at the east end of town, and numbered about half a hundred.

The strangest part was in the wind up. While the witnesses were all eagerly gazing at the lights, a cloud came from the West, which was about the size of a door, and of a grayish or smoke color. It had the form of a man standing in an upright position. As it neared the lights, it began to change its form and color, and finally assumed that of a black coffin. On passing to the east, it hovered over the field which contained the balls of light, and rested at about a distance of forty or fifty feet from the ground. The lights being in procession, a march was made around the coffin with seeming funeral tread, and when a complete circle was formed a halt was made. A lid seemed to arise from the coffin, and with slow movement, the lights entered the same, and were lost to view. The coffin like object was then wafted southward, and on reaching the graveyard, settled down and was seen no more.

A great number of our citizens witnessed that night's phenomena, which will be ever memorable.— [Brownsville Banner, 10th.

The Sedalia (Missouri) Democrat, 4-14-1875, p.2

A HORRID PHANTOM.

A White-Robed Apparition with a Gleaming Light—A Terrified Horse and Rider.

[From the Reading, Pa., Eagle.]

A thrilling affair occurred a few evenings since near Sheridan. Our informant, who has not been heretofore a believer in ghosts or hobgoblins, and who is a man of strong and steady nerve, was so unstrung by the horrid vision presented to his view that he is rather disinclined to converse on the subject. The following facts, however, were gleaned from his account of the occurrence:

He was on his way home on a rather dark and misty night, on horseback, and, as usual, without any thought of danger or of supernatural things, and when some distance this side of Sheridan he was astonished at the terror of his horse, which endeavored to turn back and seemed wild with fright. On looking ahead, a little to one side, the rider was stricken first with astonishment, then with fear, at beholding a bright light on the bank of the lonely creek, at first gleaming brilliantly and then gradually decreasing in intensity until it almost disappeared, seeming to recede as if borne backward with incredible rapidity.

Stimulated by curiosity he endeavored to approach it more closely, but his terrified horse refused to go forward, vainly struggling to turn and rush away. As the light almost disappeared in the distance the trembling animal was urged forward, and was already past the place where it had first appeared, which was some little distance from the road, when far up in a field of rising ground the light again appeared, borne by what appeared to be a human figure, clothed in white, approaching with amazing rapidity, while as it advanced, evidently gliding along the ground, the light, which it seemed to carry in one hand, blazed forth with fast increasing brilliancy.

What it was like he could not exactly say, but it was something shadowy and indistinct, and yet horrible and ghastly in the extreme. Horse and rider were motionless with wonder and curiosity, but when the horrible phantom had approached within about a hundred yards terror became master, and the frightened horse sprung forward with a burst of speed that almost unseated his master, and stopped not until he was at his own stable door, when he was quickly put within and the man, without mentioning the matter even to his wife, hastened to bed and spent a sleepless night.

His haggard appearance next day caused inquiry, and he was induced to give his account of the matter to an Eagle representative. It is hinted that a horrible tragedy once occurred near the haunted spot, and that the phantom is seen once every fifty years. How much truth there is in this latter statement our informant was unable to say; but he intends to leave the investigation to some one else, having had enough of ghosts for a long time to come.

The Cincinnati Daily Star, 1-15-1876, p.2

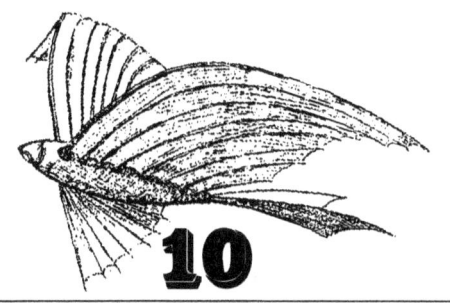

10
GHOST OR HIGH TECH HUMANOID?

January 12, 1876
Sheridan, Pennsylvania

ALTHOUGH THIS NEXT STORY is often viewed as a bit of a "ghost tale," it appears to actually be an encounter with an otherworldly humanoid figure who was dressed in a high-tech suit, who "glided" instead of walked, and who carried a powerful handheld light source. The incident happened in early January 1876 in the woods near Sheridan, Pennsylvania. A report of the case appeared in many newspapers, including the *Reading (PA) Eagle*, the *St. Louis (MO) Globe-Democrat*, and the *Cincinnati (OH) Daily Star*.

The article begins by explaining that this strange encounter was experienced by "our informant, who has not been heretofore a believer in ghosts or hobgoblins, and who is a man of strong and steady nerve...." This particular encounter with a bizarre humanoid, however, completely unnerved the gentleman to the extent that he was "disinclined to converse on the subject." The reporter managed to piece together the essence of what the witness had experienced, which he related in the newspaper account.

Illustration Accompanying Original Article

The witness, on horseback, was on his way home "on a rather dark and misty night," when suddenly his horse became very nervous and seemingly terrified. The rider struggled to keep the horse, which was "wild with fright," from turning back the way they had come.

Suddenly, the witness noticed a very bright light on the bank of a nearby lonely creek. The illumination at first was intense and kept increasing in brightness.

OLD WEST UFOS: 1865-1895

Wanting to get a closer look at the source of the light, the witness fought to coax his horse to move in the direction of the anomaly, but the terrified animal refused to move. At that point, the brightness of the light began to diminish until it nearly went out, and the horse finally began moving forward.

They moved to where the figure had first appeared, alongside a creek, but it was no longer there. The humanoid shape had moved up an embankment and was quite a distance away when the bright light returned. The witness said, "The light again appeared, borne by what appeared to be a human figure, clothed in white, approaching with amazing rapidity, while as it advanced, evidently gliding along the ground, the light, which it seemed to carry in one hand, blazed forth with fast, increasing brilliancy."

The witness described the figure as "something shadowy and indistinct." Although human-like, the creature's identity could not be clearly ascertained. The eerie shape approached to within 100 yards of the witness when the frightened horse suddenly sprang forward with a burst of speed that almost threw off the rider. Setting a furious pace, the horse did not stop until it arrived at its own stable door.

Terrified and exhausted by the ordeal, the witness told nobody what had happened, not even his wife, and went right to bed that evening. On the following day, his "haggard appearance" was such that he was finally persuaded to tell his story to others, including to a reporter from the *Reading Eagle* newspaper of Reading, Pennsylvania.

THE REAL COWBOYS & ALIENS

U.S. Soldier Engaged in Radiation Experiment

So, the question remains -- who was the shadowy figure that apparently had access to technology far beyond what was available in 1876? Other than dim, flickering lanterns, there were no sources of light that could be held in one's hand in 1876, and certainly nothing that could generate an intense beam of light that seemed to illuminate the whole area of the sighting. Also, what was the significance of the "gliding" motion of the stranger, coupled with the fact that it was able to move so incredibly fast? It seems plausible that the humanoid was using a type of personal transportation device similar to a small electric scooter or other personal transporter.

And what of the stranger's striking white clothing that somehow seemed to hide the features and characteristics of the body, suggesting it was a type of suit, perhaps a space suit or a biohazard suit? To someone familiar with cases where witnesses have encountered humanoid entities during a UFO sighting, the description given by the gentleman from 1876 seems to fit perfectly.

Could the strange humanoid have been a space traveler whose ship had landed nearby? Could he have been a time traveler, holding in his hand the tools of the future while carrying out a research mission on a bygone era? Whatever the answer might be, clearly this was not a disembodied spirit, but rather, a humanoid being that was accidentally discovered while skulking around in a dark forest at night, carrying out experiments, specimen collection, or observations. Startled and with his mission potentially compromised, the mysterious figure took steps to end the confrontation, possibly by causing fright to both the human and his horse. In the end, he was successful.

THE REAL COWBOYS & ALIENS

Stationary Meteors.

To the Editor of the Scientific American:

A few minutes after ten o'clock on Friday evening, September 7, 1877, Mr. John Graham, of Bloomington, Ind., had his attention arrested by a sudden light in the heavens, and on looking up he saw a stationary meteor between *Aquila* and *Anser et Vulpecula*, about R. A. 295°, declination 15° N. It increased in brightness for a second or more, and disappeared within less than half a degree east of the point in which it was first seen. Immediately after the extinction of the first, three others, separated by intervals of three or four seconds, appeared and vanished in the same place, with the exception that one disappeared about as much west of the radiant as the first did to the east of it. Mr. Graham's curiosity was excited, and he continued to watch till, after an interval of a few minutes, a fifth meteor, corresponding in appearance to the preceding, was seen in the same place. The meteors were about equal to stars of the first magnitude. The facts indicate that a stream of meteoric matter was moving at the time almost exactly towards the observer. Two or three isolated instances of stationary meteors have been recorded; the phenomena of the 7th inst. are, however, quite extraordinary.

I have stated the observations as given me by Mr. Graham, who pointed out the position in which the meteors were seen.   DANIEL KIRKWOOD.

Bloomington, Ind.

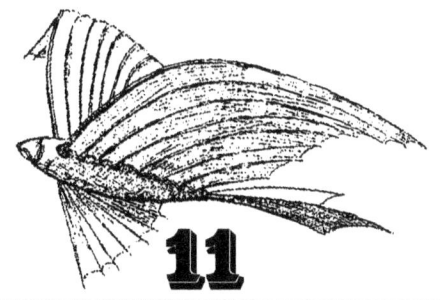

11
ASTRONOMER SPOTS FIVE UFOS

September 7, 1877
Bloomington, Indiana

SIGHTINGS BY ASTRONOMERS, whether amateurs or professionals, are considered to be among the most valid of UFO reports, and the same can be said even of astronomers of the nineteenth century, such as John Graham, an amateur, and Daniel Kirkwood, a renowned astronomer of his time who called this sighting "quite extraordinary."

It was reported in the September 29, 1877 issue of *Scientific American* that Graham had spotted five mysterious "stationary meteors" in the sky over Bloomington, Indiana.

Graham observed the first of the objects a little after 10 p.m. while looking about 40 degrees above his eastern horizon, between the constellations

THE REAL COWBOYS & ALIENS

Aquila and Vulpecula, just above and to the left of the bright star Altair.

The first object shone brightly and seemed to increase in brightness as it traveled slightly to the right. Then it suddenly dimmed and went out, after which four more bright objects appeared at various times in the same general area, mostly appearing one at a time, disappearing, and then being replaced by another. Graham stated that the brightness of the objects was equivalent to a "first magnitude" (1.0) star, which means they were similar in brightness to the nearby star Altair (magnitude 0.93).

The Star Altair - Magnitude 0.93

OLD WEST UFOS: 1865-1895

The observation was submitted to Professor Daniel Kirkwood of Indiana University at Bloomington for analysis. Kirkwood, according to the *Indianapolis Journal*, was an expert "concerning astronomical subjects." Kirkwood, who later taught at Stanford, is credited for a number of important discoveries, including "Kirkwood's Gaps," concerning the orbits of asteroids around the sun.

Kirkwood Observatory in Bloomington, Indiana

In 1881, Kirkwood was at the center of an effort to have the state of Indiana fund construction of an astronomical observatory in Bloomington, and a local newspaper said, "The State has the astronomer for the place in the person of Daniel Kirkwood of the University of Bloomington, a man of great learning and worth - the Proctor of America. And his vast learning, talents and great worth to the State of Indiana should not be lost for the want of an observatory ...." [*Hamilton County*

THE REAL COWBOYS & ALIENS

Democrat (Noblesville, Indiana) 2-4-1881, p. 3] The observatory was built in 1900, five years after the professor's death, and was named the Kirkwood Observatory.

Kirkwood's opinion about Graham's sighting of five mysterious objects was that the objects were possibly "meteoric material," that was moving toward the Earth from outer space, causing it to appear to be virtually stationary in the sky. However, Kirkwood leaves the door open to alternate explanations, stating, "... the phenomena of the 7th inst. are, however, quite extraordinary."

UFO researchers have an entirely different theory for what Graham saw that night. They believe the witness saw five UFOs inbound to the Earth from some unknown point of origin in outer space. Clearly, the objects were unusual and unexpected, given their location in the night sky and their appearance and motion. The sighting was "extraordinary" enough to draw the attention of the very conservative editors of the *Scientific American*, who elected to publish Professor Kirkman's letter about the phenomenon. In the end, Kirkman's theory that it was meteors that were moving toward the Earth may not be the correct explanation. As the original witness stated, the remarkable sight at first "arrested" his attention, and then when he discovered more objects in the same place, he said his curiosity was "greatly excited."

U.S. Census Bureau records indicate that the original eyewitness, John Graham, was an attorney at law who lived on "Rail Road Street" in

Bloomington. He was approximately 33 years of age at the time of the sighting.

1880 U.S. Census Showing Attorney John Graham

Although his father, who was 77, was also called John, it seems more likely that the son was the one who made the astronomical observation. His dad was a carpenter originally from Ireland, and obviously the younger Graham had the higher level of education and, most likely, greater curiosity about the stars. That is our assumption, in any event.

In conclusion, this was a remarkable astronomical observation that leaves us wondering what type of space craft might have been approaching the Earth on that quiet November evening.

*Artist Neil Riebe's Depiction
of 1878 Flying Saucer*

12
THE FARMER AND THE FLYING SAUCER

January 22, 1878
Dallas, Texas

STRANGE FLYING SHIPS seen in the sky weren't called "flying saucers" until the late 1940s -- or so we thought. Long before that, in 1878, a farmer in Dallas, Texas, saw something in the sky that he described as a "large saucer." It was in fact, the first time in history that the word "saucer" was used for a UFO.

The farmer, John Martin, was hunting on his property six miles north of Dallas. It was morning on Tuesday, January 22, 1878, when suddenly, Martin noticed a dark object in the sky to the south. When the farmer first saw it, the UFO was about the size of an orange, but it grew in size rapidly as it approached his position. The local newspaper said, "The peculiar shape and velocity with which the object seemed to approach riveted his attention and he strained his eyes to discover its character." Since it was morning and yet the object looked dark, it seems that the UFO did not have any lights. Instead, it appeared as a dark shape against the bright blue of the sky. Martin kept staring at it as it moved rapidly toward him. He later said the UFO "appeared to be going through space at wonderful speed."

The brightness of the sky temporarily blinded Martin, and he lost track of where the object was. He rested his eyes for a few moments, and by the time he could see again, the UFO was right on top of him, and it was much larger than before.

Daylight Disc Sighting
(Courtesy UFOcasebook.com)

An article about Martin's sighting appeared in the *Dallas (Texas) Daily Herald* on January 23,

OLD WEST UFOS: 1865-1895

1878 on page 4, which stated, "When directly over him it was about the size of a large saucer and was evidently at great height." So, although it was huge in size, it was also very high up in the sky. This means its true size was even larger than what it seemed to be.

Martin described the shape of the object as sort of like a balloon. But, although hot-air balloons already existed, they obviously did not move very fast and they were rarely seen in the skies of North Texas.

Martin kept watching the UFO until it moved completely out of view. "It went as rapidly as it had come and was soon lost to sight in the heavenly skies," the newspaper said.

In addition to appearing in the *Dallas Daily Herald*, the sighting was also mentioned in the *Denison (Texas) Daily News* on January 25, 1878. The article, titled "A Strange Phenomenon," consisted entirely of a first-hand report from Farmer Martin. On the following page is the original version of the article, taken from the Dallas newspaper.

The newspaper reporter confirms that Martin was a trustworthy eyewitness and not the kind of person who would make up a false story. "Mr. Martin is a gentleman of undoubted veracity and this strange occurrence, if it was not a balloon, deserves the attention of our scientists," the article said.

In the early 1970s, Dr. J. Allen Hynek, the famous astronomer and UFO investigator, studied the Martin sighting. Hynek classified the incident

THE REAL COWBOYS & ALIENS

as a "daylight disc," which is a type of UFO seen in daytime that travels very fast and makes almost no sound. These daylight discs are also sometimes seen making sudden, sharp turns without slowing down at all.

J. Allen Hynek
(U.S. Government Photo)

Daylight discs are often described as shiny or metallic, they usually display no lights, and sometimes, witnesses may hear a very faint "swishing" sound. Daylight discs were mostly reported after 1940, which makes this 1878 sighting extremely rare. It remains one of the most interesting UFO cases of the 1800s.

> **A Strange Phenomenon.**
> From Mr. John Martin, a farmer who lives some six miles north of this city, we learn the following strange story: Tuesday morning, while out hunting, his attention was directed to a dark object high up in the northern sky. The peculiar shape, and the velocity with which the object seemed to approach, riveted his attention, and he strained his eyes to discover its character. When first noticed it appeared to be about the size of an orange, which continued to grow in size. After gazing at it for some time, Mr. Martin became blind from long looking, and left off viewing it for a time, in order to rest his eyes. On resuming his view the object was almost overhead and had increased considerably in size and appeared to be going through space at a wonderful speed. When directly over him it was about the size of a large saucer, and was evidently at a great height. Mr. Martin thought that it resembled, as well as he could judge at such a distance, a balloon, which seemed to him to be the most reasonable solution of the strange phenomena, though he is of the opinion that it was possibly some of the heavenly bodies. It went as rapidly as it had come and was soon lost to sight in the southern sky. Mr. Martin is a gentleman of undoubted veracity, and this strange occurrence, if it was not a balloon, deserves the attention of our scientists.

Dallas Daily Herald, 1-23-1878, p.4

DRONES IN THE 19TH CENTURY?

February 1878
Osceola Township, Iowa

IN OUR TIME, remote controlled drone aircraft are commonplace, used in all industries, by the military, and even by private individuals for recreation. A wonder of technology, these small vessels carry sophisticated cameras and other equipment, can maneuver into very tight spaces, and can hover in place to facilitate photography or remote observation. Modern drones can also carry a high-intensity light attachment that illuminates dark areas around the craft. Had drone technology been available in the nineteenth century, what an amazing impact it would have had in all human endeavors. The country that had such technology would have ruled the world.

But what if drones did somehow find their way back into the nineteenth century? There are several intriguing UFO cases from the 1800s that describe small, hovering objects that followed people around, moving up into the sky and back down at will, causing terror and confusion among the populace. It seems obvious to us of the twenty-first century that these small, highly maneuverable flying objects were very likely a form of advanced, remote-controlled drone aircraft.

Typical Drone in 2019 (Public Domain)

One of the most striking examples from the 1800s of sightings of this type occurred in Osceola Township, Iowa, in 1878. The newspapers of the period record that the local citizens were plagued by a strange, hovering light that tended to follow them around town. Since the object was brightly lit, it was called "a haunted locomotive headlight ... without any visible means of support."

The full account of the case was first published in the *Ackley (Iowa) Enterprise* of February 8, 1878, and it began like this: "A young man well known in the community and regarded of undoubted veracity, relates that he was going home

OLD WEST UFOS: 1865-1895

across the fields from a neighbor's when his attention was attracted by a light moving along the road at some distance from him."

> —Osceola township is stirring up the whole of Franklin county with the story of a haunted locomotive headlight, which goes traveling around the prairies without any visible means of support or the slightest provocation.

Weekly Davenport (Iowa) Democrat,
2-14-1878, p. 1

"He thought at first that the light proceeded from a lantern, carried by someone traveling the highway, but as it approached nearer, he noticed that it was much larger than a lantern. When the light reached a point in the road nearly opposite him, it stopped and came directly toward him with great velocity, until it was within a few feet of him when it stopped. The observer describes it as about the size of a half bushel and of intense brightness. It then rose in the air a distance of several rods [1 rod = 16.5 feet] and then to descend where the gentleman stood."

The maneuvers described by the witness -- the object rapidly ascending and descending -- sound exactly like those of a modern drone carrying a spotlight attachment. Interestingly, the witness at first thought someone was walking along the road carrying a lantern, only to realize that the light was hovering unsupported by any means.

It is also interesting that the drone seemed unaware of the man until it came within a short distance of him. Suddenly sensing his presence, the object shot toward him at a very rapid rate, coming to a stop only a few feet in front of him.

The object itself was described as "about the size of a half bushel and of intense brightness."

After the object came to a stop a few feet from the witness, this is what happened next: "He says that he is not usually easily frightened, but he could not account for the strange sight and he retraced his steps to the house he had just left. The light followed him until he reached the house when it went off a short distance and he lost sight of it."

At this point, the object seemed to have zoomed out of sight, either straight up into the air or up above the roof of the house. The scared witness entered his friends' house and asked two of them to accompany him as he again made his way back home. They agreed to do so.

The three young men then stepped out of the house and looked around but could not locate the strange object. Heading back along the path to the original witness' house, the group suddenly saw the object come back into view. It was witnessed by all three young men this time.

The narrative continued, "[The object] did not come so close as before but would suddenly disappear and soon come in sight again in an entirely different direction and at a considerable distance from where it was last seen."

In the close of the article, the reporter reveals that this phenomenon had been seen in Osceola Township before by other witnesses. "The light was also seen by the people at a number of houses in the neighborhood. None of those who were witnesses of the strange occurrence are able to give any explanation of the phenomenon. That they are all honest in the recital of what they saw is conceded by all who know the parties. We venture no explanation."

The strange event was mentioned in a number of other newspapers of the time, including the *Ottumwa (Iowa) Weekly Courier*, *The Des Moines (Iowa) Register*, and the *Quad-City Times* of Davenport, Iowa.

What was this mysterious hovering object that terrorized the citizens of Osceola Township in 1878? Until drone technology became common in the twenty-first century, UFO researchers had difficulty understanding what this object may have been. Now, they understand it was most likely an unmanned, remote-controlled drone vehicle. Controlled by whom and for what purpose? That we do not know.

Ackley (Iowa) Enterprise, 2-8-1878, p. 1

THE REAL COWBOYS & ALIENS

SIGHTING THE "GHOST SHIP."

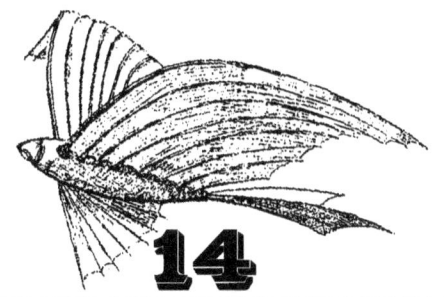

14
PROSPECTOR ABDUCTED BY GHOST SHIP

Mid 1878, Indio, California,

WHAT, YOU MAY ASK, does a "ghost ship" sighting have to do with UFOs? Well first, this ghost ship was seen flying across the sky instead of sailing out at sea, and supposedly, one of the persons who saw the flying ship may have subsequently been abducted by whatever entities manifested the apparition.

Ghost ship sightings were a common staple of sailor lore, but they usually took place at sea, not in the skies, as happened in this case. This is also an especially intriguing story because it involves some of the well-known, tried-and-true themes of all good Western folklore, including prospectors, mining for treasure, a ghostly apparition, and the unforgiving desert.

THE REAL COWBOYS & ALIENS

The story in this chapter appeared in the November 3, 1889 edition of the *San Francisco (California) Examiner*, on page 13, in an article titled "The Phantom Vessel. A Regular 'Flying Dutchman' Seen on the Colorado Desert."

The story begins in Yuma, Arizona, late in the summer of 1878 when two German prospectors stumbled into town in a haggard and frenzied condition, excitedly proclaiming that a strange flying vessel had appeared over the desert and had kidnapped one of their comrades, taking him away into the clouds!

Gold Prospectors c.1889 (Library of Congress)

The *Examiner* reported, "Late in the summer of 1878, several years after the story of the discovery of the remains of a ship had been made public, two German prospectors reached Yuma from the Colorado desert. They were in a state of great distress and reported the loss of a companion on the desert. The prospectors, it seems, had been skirting the south and west sides of the San Bernardino range in search of minerals, and their companion was lost some six days before at a point about one hundred miles northwest from Yuma. The peculiar feature of their story was their associating with and attributing the disappearance of their comrade to an apparition which they had beheld the previous evening."

The amazing narrative from the two exhausted prospectors continued in this manner: "About sundown, so the Germans said, and while encamped on the desert, they saw, at a short distance, an immense ship under full sail, which appeared to float before them as a cloud. She was of different form of construction from any vessel they had ever seen and was complicated and fantastic in her rigging."

Traditional Ghost Ship Illustration

THE REAL COWBOYS & ALIENS

What the Prospectors Saw Was Probably Similar to the Airships Seen in 1896 & 1897

In this part of the story, the witnesses describe what sounds like an ocean-going vessel ("an immense ship under full sail"), but they are careful to point out that the ship was of a totally "different form of construction" and that its rigging was "complicated and fantastic." Being of limited education and vocabulary, the witnesses were clearly struggling to understand and explain what they saw hovering in the sky above them. Clearly not a typical sailing ship, it was probably more akin to the mysterious airships that were sighted all over America in the late 1890s.

The *Examiner* article continued, "Their description of the vessel was by no means lucid, but they were very positive that their companion had been shanghaied and taken off on the 'ghost ship,' as they insisted on calling it."

This is the most fascinating part of the story – that the men believed their companion had been abducted by whatever entities were aboard the mysterious hovering airship. Although they did not give a detailed explanation of why they blamed the disappearance of their companion on the airship, it was clear that they felt the man had been "taken" ["shanghaied"] by the occupants of the bizarre ship.

Original Article with Illustration

The prospectors' strange story concluded as follows: "The story of the Germans was received with a good deal of contempt by the people of Yuma, who, after telling the prospectors that they were double adjective fools, sent two men and

three Indian trailers on the train to Indio to search the desert east of that station for the missing man. The second day, his naked corpse was found about forty miles from the railroad, with the scorching rays of the sun falling upon it. He had died in the desert of thirst, but no sign of the phantom ship was seen."

The fact that the missing German was found dead and without a stitch of clothing on him has led some researchers to believe that he was abducted, possibly experimented on, and then dumped unceremoniously back onto the hot desert sand without clothing, food, or water, which was, in effect, a death sentence. In UFO literature, there have been other cases where an abductee is returned to Earth sans clothing.

The story of the phantom airship and the abducted German prospector became quite the sensation in the North American newspapers, appearing in numerous papers in California, Nebraska, Kansas, Montana, North Dakota, and elsewhere. The earliest appearance of the article we could locate, however, was the previously mentioned *San Francisco Examiner* story of November 3, 1889.

Was this 1878 case a very early example of alien abduction? It certainly seems to bear all the hallmarks of that uncanny phenomenon. If such, it precedes all the known cases in the annals of Ufology!

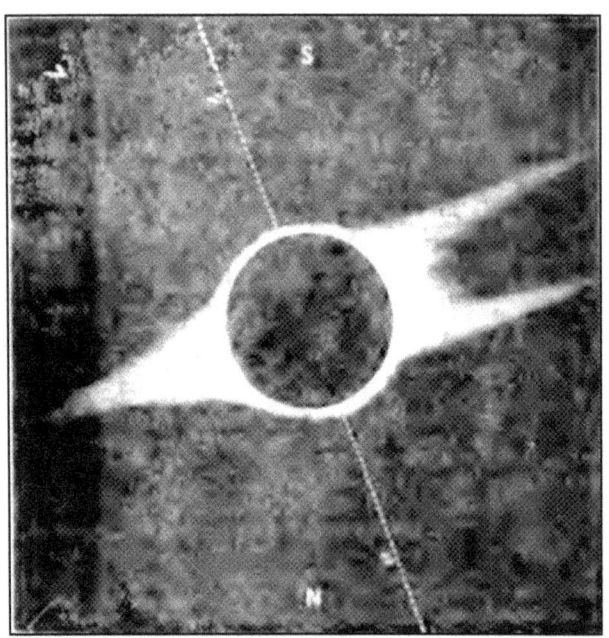

Photo of Solar Eclipse Taken by Watson on July 28, 1878

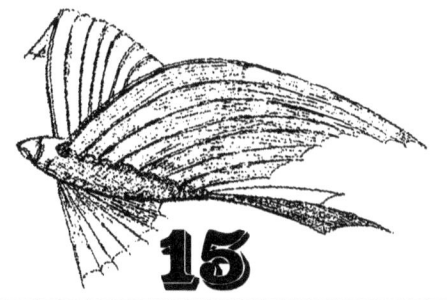

SHINING SPHERE OF THE SUN

July 28, 1878
Rawlins, Wyoming

IN THIS CHAPTER, we will discuss an 1878 observation by astronomers in Wyoming of a mysterious shining sphere near the sun. Its importance is clear in relation to a number of recent sightings of strange objects near the sun. Among these newer cases is a massive, cylindrical object called Oumaumua that passed through our solar system in 2017, zipping past the sun at 196,000 miles per hour before yanking free of the sun's gravitational pull and moving out into the far reaches of space. Some astronomers, among them Harvard's Avi Loeb, proposed that Oumaumua could have been an "alien spacecraft."

Oumaumua (NASA Illustration)

Other recent sightings of objects in the vicinity of the sun have similarly caused great agitation. On April 24, 2012, NASA's Solar and Heliospheric Observatory (SOHO) spotted an anomalous object seemingly orbiting the sun at fairly close range. NASA blamed it on cosmic rays striking the camera causing momentary photographic artifacts. However, some researchers were not buying that explanation, believing the object was a UFO either observing our sun or drawing energy from it.

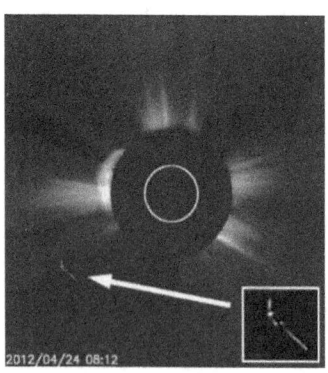

OLD WEST UFOS: 1865-1895

Then again on July 24, 2019, the SOHO cameras snapped an image that seemed unexplainable – a bizarre object near the sun that was ten times the size of planet Earth. UFO researcher Scott C. Waring captured the image from a NASA web site before it became mysteriously unavailable.

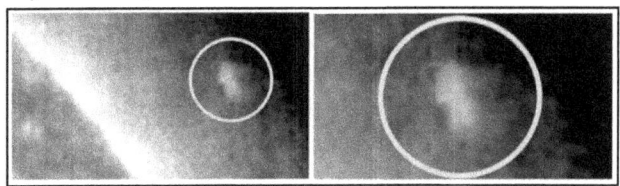

2019 Photos Captured from SOHO
(Courtesy Scott C. Waring)

The history of strange objects near the sun goes all the way back to year 1878, when a group of astronomers in Wyoming discovered a silvery sphere near the sun. During observation of a solar eclipse on July 28, 1878, several astronomers spotted the mysterious sphere between the planet Mercury and the sun. At first, they thought it might be a star and later a planet, but neither explanation seemed to really fit. Astronomers had previously theorized that a planet, which they called "Vulcan," should exist within Mercury's orbit; therefore, the strange object seen in 1878 was believed to possibly be this enigmatic planet. In the prestigious science magazine *Nature* on August 29, 1878, the renowned British astronomer J. Norman Lockyer said, "There is little doubt, I think, that an intra-Mercuria planet has been found by Prof. [James Craig] Watson. If it will fit one of Leverrier's orbits, and should turn out to be Vulcan, no doubt astronomers will be able to keep a firm grasp upon it, and sooner or later its elements will be determined."

Astronomer J. Norman Lockyer (Left) and Professor Craig Watson (Right)

As it turned out, what the scientists discovered was a huge mystery that remains to this day. If not a star or planet, then an unidentified object orbiting the sun seems a very real possibility.

The story of the discovery began as Lockyer travelled to America to accompany Watson and another astronomer, Professor Simon Newcomb, as they went planet hunting during the solar eclipse of 1878. As Watson and Newcomb set up their equipment and made their observations, Lockyer furiously took notes which he would later publish in the magazine he founded, *Nature*.

Lockyer wrote, "Prof. Watson ... broke off work on a planet beyond Neptune to come to discover one inside Mercury. He went with me in Mr. Silvis' railway photographic car from Rawlins to Separation on the morning of the eclipse, intending to observe with me at the station we were determined to occupy, with our light equipment, as the number of detached clouds visible at the time of totality on previous days had strongly shown the advantage of separating the parties as much as possible."

Professor Simon Newcomb

"We chose a spot to leeward of one of the enormous water tanks of the Union Pacific Railway, which form the chief features in the interesting but desolate plains in that region, over which the wind sweeps at times with incredible violence."

The two astronomers rode a specially equipped photographic railway car invented by J. B. Silvis of the Union Pacific Railroad. Their objective was to find an optimum spot, not plagued by cloud cover, somewhere along the route between Rawlins and Separation.

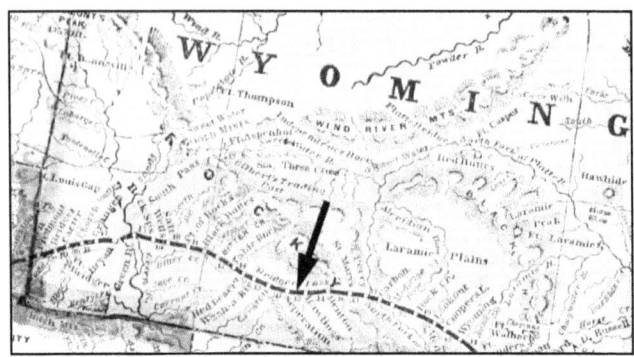

1875 Map of the Area Where the Observation was Made

Lockyer wrote, "On reaching our destination, we found Prof. Newcomb, whose camp was about a mile away, and it was then agreed that as both he and Prof. Watson were to hunt for the planet, they had better be together...."

Lockyer learned later that Watson and Newcomb had quickly begun operations to locate new planets at their improvised camp. With the assistance of a carpenter hired from the nearby town of Rawlins, Watson constructed a special equatorial mount for his telescope that would allow him to more easily mark the locations of astronomical objects around the sun.

Watson started his observations to the left of the sun's disc and then slowly swept to the right, making note of objects that he discovered along the path.

*Photographic Train Car of J. B. Silvis, 1874
(Courtesy Union Pacific Railroad)*

THE REAL COWBOYS & ALIENS

While carefully surveying the area around the sun, taking advantage of the eclipse, he suddenly found the unexplained sphere just to the right and slightly below the sun.

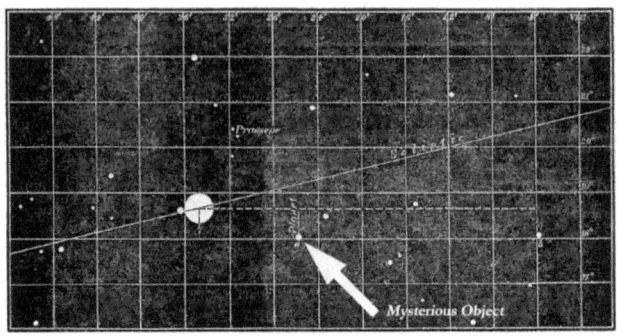

Chart Showing a Mysterious Silver Sphere Near the Sun

Lockyer wrote, "[Watson] commenced operations to the left of the sun and saw the stars marked, but none others. Then sweeping out to the star marked *b*, he noticed on his return another not on the chart, marked *a*. He then made three marks on his right ascension paper circle, on the spots occupied by the pointer, when the sun, *a* and *b*, were successively brought into the center of the field. He next determined the difference of declination in the same way between the sun and *a*, having the additional help that *a* was nearly in the same declination as *b*."

After returning to his home in England, Lockyer found out that another astronomer had possibly seen the strange object. Astronomer Lewis A. Swift of Rochester, New York, who later became director of California's Mount Lowe Observatory, spotted "two stars not down in the charts or star maps, and about as bright as the pole star." Lockyer said, "... about one minute after the commencement of totality, two stars caught his (Mr. Swift's) eye about three degrees, by estimation, southwest of the sun."

"The stars were both of the fifth magnitude, and but one is on the chart of the heavens. This star he recognized as Theta in Cancer. The two stars were about eight minutes apart. There is no such configuration of stars in the constellation of Cancer."

Since only one of these two stars could be identified, Lockyer surmised that "the star Mr. Swift saw may have been the same that was seen by Prof. Watson, who was located at Rawlins."

As in more recent sightings of strange objects near the sun, the 1878 sighting by two noted astronomers continues to be of great interest to UFO researchers. Although scientists have not ruled out the possibility that "planetoids" might exist between Mercury and the sun, there seem to be no other plausible explanation for what Watson and Swift saw through their telescopes in 1878.

Was there a UFO in orbit around the sun? If so, what could be its purpose? After recent sightings of similar objects, UFO researchers have conjectured that these craft are harvesting energy from the solar sphere to use for propulsion or other purposes. Alternately, these craft may be conducting research on the sun. What the truth of the 1878 sighting really is may never be known, but the evidence seems clear that the object seen by Watson and Swift was not a planet or star.

> There is little doubt, I think, that an intra-Mercurial planet has been found by Prof. Watson. If it will fit one of Leverrier's orbits, and should turn out to be Vulcan, no doubt astronomers will be able to keep a firm grasp upon it, and sooner or later its elements will be determined.
>
> Prof. Watson, of Ann Arbor, whose belt, as the papers here put it, is graced with the scalps of I know not how many minor planets, broke off work on a planet beyond Neptune to come to discover one inside Mercury. He went with me in Mr. Silvis' railway photographic car from Rawlins to Separation on the morning of the eclipse, intending to observe with me at the station we were determined to occupy, with our light equipments, as the number of detached clouds visible at the time of totality on the previous days had strongly shown the advantage of separating the parties as much as possible. We chose a spot to leeward of one of the enormous water tanks of the Union Pacific Railway, which form the chief features in the interesting but desolate plains in that region, over which the wind sweeps at times with incredible violence.
>
> On reaching our destination we found Prof. Newcomb, whose camp was about a mile away, and it was then agreed that as both he and Prof. Watson were to hunt for the planet they had better be together, so I lost his company during the eclipse.
>
> Prof. Watson's plan of operation was to sweep south of the sun and observe all the stars in the map, a part of which is here reproduced (Fig. 6), and to refer the position of any new body to the stars, or, if possible, to the sun itself. For this purpose, with the assistance of the Rawlins carpenter, he armed his equatorial with paper circles and brass wire pointers. He commenced operations to the left of the sun and saw the stars marked, but none others. Then sweeping out to the star marked b he noticed on his return another not on the chart, marked a. He then made three marks on his right ascension paper circle, on the spots occupied by the pointer, when the sun, a and b, were successively brought into the centre of the field He next determined the difference of declination in the same way between the sun and a, having the additional help that a was nearly in the same declination as b. He then repeated his R.A. measures, and called Prof. Newcomb, but the eclipse was over before anything more could be done. I give this statement from memory only (as I was too busy to make notes at the time), as I heard it soon after the eclipse at the camp, before the telescope was dismounted. It is probable that subsequent careful measures of the circles may alter the place—
>
> R.A. 8h. 26m.
> Dec. + 18° 00'.
>
> I telegraphed to you, somewhat, but the alteration will be small.
>
> Since arriving here I have learned that Mr. Swift, of Rochester, a well tried observer, also saw the planet The first account I read of his work was as follows:—
>
> "This gentleman made a very careful search for Vulcan, scanning the heavens very closely with his splendid comet eye-piece, made by the celebrated Gundlach, but he saw nothing of it. He did, however, see about three degrees from the sun, two stars not down in the charts or star maps, and about as bright as the pole star—they were pointing directly towards the sun. On attempting to re-find them, he was prevented by a little cloud."
>
> Since then, however, another fuller account of his work has appeared, from which I gather that about one minute after the commencement of totality two stars caught his (Mr. Swift's) eye about three degrees, by estimation, south west of the sun. He saw them twice, and attempted third observation, but a small cloud obscured the locality. The stars were both of the fifth magnitude, and but one is on the chart of the heavens. This star he recognise as Theta in Cancer. The two stars were about eight minutes apart. There is no such configuration of star

Nature Magazine, 8-29-1878

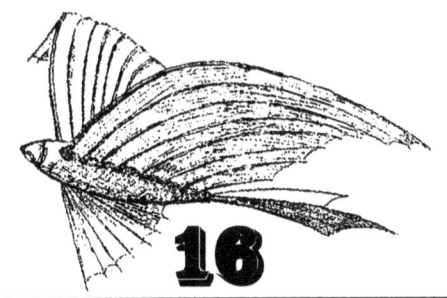

16
PHANTOM TRAIN OR UFO?

July 30, 1878
Edwardsville, Kansas

THE OLD WEST was replete with stories about spectral trains that would suddenly appear along lonely stretches of tracks or even where railroad lines were long abandoned or nonexistent. A ghostly train whistle would be followed by the loud noise of an oncoming locomotive, and then terrified spectators would see a shimmering, translucent train go streaking past, often vanishing into thin air right before their eyes.

In this chapter, we will examine one particular case that is often included with "ghost train" stories, but was actually not a ghost train sighting at all. Rather, it seems to have been a sighting of another one of the mysterious futuristic air or land vehicles that occasionally turned up in North America in the 1800s.

THE REAL COWBOYS & ALIENS

This story, first appearing in the *Kansas City (Kansas) Pioneer* on August 1, 1878, has a number of very unique characteristics that make it worth further study. Unlike typical ghost train encounters, this case took place in broad daylight. Twelve witnesses observed a strange craft that definitely did not look like a train travelling along the railroad tracks before it suddenly veered off the tracks and plowed through thickly-forested woods.

With the headline "A Phantom Train Tearing Down on the K. P. Road at Edwardsville," the newspaper article reported, "Edwardsville is twelve miles west of Kansas City, on the Kansas Pacific road, and has a haunted house, and has been the theater of many mysterious sights and sounds. But the following, which occurred in daylight, and to which there were a dozen eyewitnesses, is one of the most remarkable occurrences on record. Mr. Timmons, our informant, is one of the most substantial farmers and reliable men in Wyandotte County."

A search of historical records shows that J. F. Timmons was an influential landowner, farmer, and member of the political party known as the Greenbacks. According to *Wikipedia*, "The Greenback Party was an American political party with an anti-monopoly ideology which was active between 1874 and 1889. The party ran candidates in three presidential elections -- in the elections of 1876, 1880, and 1884, before fading away."

Illustration That Accompanied the Original Article

THE REAL COWBOYS & ALIENS

Railroad Crew with Handcar C.1921

Timmons told the newspaper, "Last Tuesday morning [July 30], the section men on the Kansas Pacific road on my farm, seeing the storm coming up on the track, got their handcar and started full speed for Edwardsville. They had run but a little way, when the entire crowd at the same time, saw coming around the curve east of Edwardsville, what they supposed to be a locomotive at full speed."

These "section men" were apparently doing routine maintenance on the tracks using a handcar when they became aware of what seemed to be a storm, or some kind of atmospheric disturbance, off in the distance. They got into their handcar and began heading toward the nearby town of Edwardsville. Suddenly, they heard what sounded like a locomotive coming toward them at full speed, raising the specter of a head-on crash.

Timmons continued, "They jumped down and took their car off the track as fast as possible, when they saw that it was not a locomotive. Whatever it was, it came down the track, giving off a volume of dense smoke with occasional flashes resembling a headlight in the center of the smoke." Although this story is often included with other stories about "ghost trains," it was clearly not a train. The eyewitnesses said that although it "sounded" like a train, it was definitely "not a locomotive."

Timmons continued, "It came three-fourths of a mile from where they first saw it, then turned off the track at a pile of cordwood, went round it once, then went in a southwesterly direction through a thick wood. The section men came running to my house, evidently much frightened and bewildered by what they saw. What was it?"

Bearing a striking similarity to the fictional time machine locomotive from the motion picture *Back to the Future III*, this strange vehicle spotted in 1878 remains totally unexplained even today. That it was not actually a train is very clear and that it did not require tracks upon which to move is also clear. Also interesting is that its appearance was immediately preceded by an atmospheric disturbance, perhaps the opening of a portal or wormhole, through which the strange vehicle traveled. Could it have been another instance of an object from the future or from another dimension intruding upon the unsuspecting denizens of the 19th century? Or, might it have been extraterrestrial in origin, having first landed from the sky and then moved along the most convenient "roadway," which would have been the railroad tracks?

1819 Built Locomotive (Library of Congress)

OLD WEST UFOS: 1865-1895

The newspaper account points out the uniqueness of this case, saying that the incident "which occurred in daylight, and to which there are a dozen eye-witnesses, is one of the most remarkable occurrences on record." Given the unique nature of the sighting, the event does not really lend itself to being grouped with other "phantom train" tales, which generally happened at night and were seen by only one or two witnesses.

This wasn't the only "otherworldly" train encounter that the authors dug up, though. There was another in which a glowing fireball came streaking out of the sky and slammed into a moving train! The story "The Locomotive Met a Ball of Fire," was published in the June 11, 1891 edition of the *Binghamton [New York] Herald*. The article said, "An engineer on the Delaware, Lackawanna and Western says he was coming down the Chenango valley when the recent storm burst. A vivid flash of lightning startled him, but he was not prepared for what followed. A huge ball of fire was seen on one of the rails coming rapidly toward the locomotive. He shut off steam and reversed the engine. The lightning, which looked like a ball of liquid fire about the size of a twelve inch football, struck the driving wheels of the locomotive and, after running several times around them, crossed over on the axles to the opposite side of the track and went spinning away in the direction from which it came and vanished around a distant curve. The engine was not damaged, with the exception of the glass oilers on the side rods, which were broken, and the paint on the 'driver' was blistered."

THE REAL COWBOYS & ALIENS

The fact that the paint was blistered is interesting and offered proof that the train had in fact come into contact with something highly unusual. Was the 12-inch fireball that struck the train some kind of energy beam fired from a UFO? Or perhaps it was an unmanned probe of some type that was speeding down the tracks on an unknown mission before colliding with the locomotive?

A PHANTOM TRAIN

Tearing Down on the K. P. Road, at Edwardsville,

FRIGHTENS THE SECTION MEN AND CAUSES THEM TO CLEAR THE TRACK.

It Frisks Off Around a Wood-Pile, and Disappears in the Forest, Amid Fire and Smoke.

Edwardsville is twelve miles west of Kansas City, on the K. P. road, and has a haunted house, and has been the theater of many mysterious sights and sounds. But the following which occurred in daylight, and to which there are a dozen eye witnesses, is one of the most remarkable occurences on record Mr. Timmons, our informant is one of the most substantial farmers and reliable men in Wyandott county.

Edwardsville, July 31, 1878. — Last Teusday morning, the section men on the K. P. road on my farm, seeing the storm coming up very fast, got their hand car on the track and started full speed for Edwardsville. They had run but a little ways when the entire crowd at the same time, saw coming around the curve east of Edwardsville, what they supposed to be a locomotive at full speed, they jumped down and took their car off the track as fast as possible, when they saw it was not a locomotive. What ever it was came down the track giving off a volume of dense smoke with occasional flashes resembling a head light in the center of the smoke. It came three-fourths of a mile from where they first saw it, then, turned off the track at a pile of cord wood, went around it once, then went off in a south westerly direction, through a thick wood. The section men came running to my house evidently much frightened, and bewildered by what they saw. What was it?

J. F. TIMMONS.

The Weekly Pioneer, 8-1-1878, p.4

THE JUPITER UFO

August 11 - 12, 1878
McKeesport, Pennsylvania

SOMETHING STRANGE and mysterious moved from right to left across the bright surface of the planet Jupiter beginning at 10:05 p.m. on August 11, 1878, and continued its transit for three hours and 19 minutes. It was described as a totally dark orb that reflected no light at all and much larger than the four largest moons of Jupiter which were the only ones known in 1878.

An article titled "Curious Astronomical Phenomenon" appeared in several area newspapers on August 22, 1878, stating the following:

"The *Pittsburg Chronicle* records a singular phenomenon connected with the planet Jupiter, as seen by Messrs. Gemill and Wampler, of McKeesport, Penn., with a five-inch telescope."

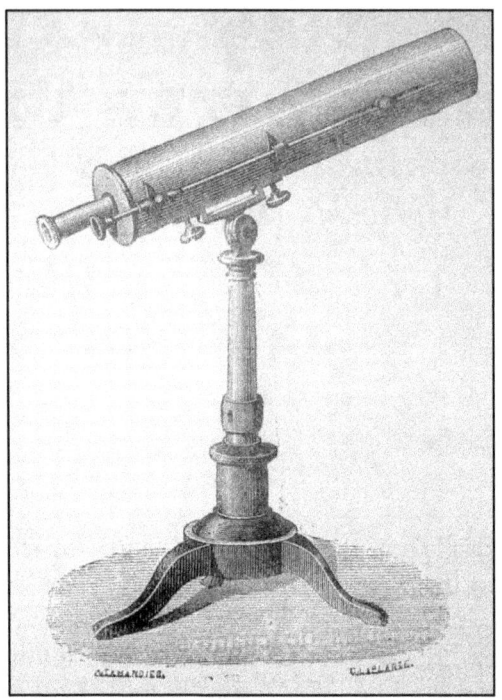

Typical Telescope, circa 1882

"At 10:05 p.m., these observers noticed on the eastern margin of the disc of Jupiter a dark round spot, just above the northern belt. It soon moved rapidly westward, just touching the belt and parallel with Jupiter's equator, and passed off the face of the planet at 1:24 a.m. of the 12th."

"Its appearance while passing across the disc of Jupiter was that of a perfect sphere or globe much larger than any of Jupiter's satellites. It appeared to stand out in space between the planet and the observer, was well and sharply defined, and most intensely black. It reflected no light and was not seen either before or after its passage across the planet."

NASA Image of Jupiter with Dark Spot Added

"It could not have been a spot on the globe of Jupiter, for it passed over its disc from first internal contact to last external contact of margins in three hours and nineteen minutes. It was not a satellite [moon] nor the shadow of one, because all the four satellites were in full view the whole time."

"It will be interesting to know whether other observers witnessed this curious transit."

Here is another case where amateur astronomers looking through a telescope discover an object where no object should exist. In this sighting, the sphere could not have been a moon of Jupiter, because the planet's four largest moons had already been discovered, and the object seen by the witnesses was far larger than the largest moon.

Simulated Transit of Venus Across Jupiter, As Happened in 1918

Planets do occasionally move across the surface of other planets, as in the 1918 transit of Venus across Jupiter. However, scientists say there are only 18 mutual planetary transits and occultations as seen from Earth between the years 1700 and 2200 - and none of them happened in 1878.

So, what was the strange shape that crossed the surface of Jupiter and how close was it to the surface of the Earth? On the question of how close it was, if the object was in orbit around the Earth, it

OLD WEST UFOS: 1865-1895

would have had to have been extremely huge to have shown up as such a large spot moving across Jupiter. However, the fact that the object seems to be a totally dark spot, displaying no surface features of any kind, leads one to believe that it was much farther away from Earth's orbit. In reviewing the 1918 transit of Venus across Jupiter, the size of Venus may be close to the size of the object that Wampler and Gemill saw, indicating a very large sphere, possibly almost planet or moon sized.

The historical record does not seem to indicate that any other observers noticed this astronomical spectacle, even though it lasted over three hours, which is another odd part of this puzzle. Perhaps this suggests that the viewing was localized – in other words, a large, black, featureless object moving in the sky between the telescope and the planet Jupiter. The problem with this theory is that the witnesses did not say that they viewed the object with the naked eye; so, the assumption is that they did not.

When investigating a sighting like this, it is important to research the identities of all persons mentioned in the contemporary reports in order to help establish the truthfulness of what happened. Regarding the identity of the two witnesses, 1880 U.S. Census Bureau data shows three male adults living in McKeesport, Pennsylvania, with the last name "Wampler." 77-year-old Joseph was an optician, 35-year-old William was a lumber merchant, and 53-year-old John was a lawyer. The census did not list any residents with the last name "Gemill"; however, persons with the surname of

"Gemmel" were very common in the region. It often happened that newspaper reporters misspelled the names of persons they interviewed. In the end, this reported sighting from Pennsylvania remains the only known evidence of a strange object that moved across the surface of Jupiter on August 11, 1878. Below is the original newspaper article, as it appeared on August 22:

> **CURIOUS ASTRONOMICAL PHENOMENON**
> *The Pittsburg Chronicle* records a singular phenomenon connected with the planet Jupiter, as seen by Messrs. Gemill and Wampler, of McKeesport, Penn., with a five-inch telescope. At 10:05 P.M., these observers noticed on the eastern margin of the disc of Jupiter a dark round spot, just above the northern belt. It soon moved rapidly westward, just touching the belt and parallel with Jupiter's equator, and passed off the face of the planet at 1:24 A.M., of the 12th. Its appearance while passing across the disc of Jupiter was that of a perfect sphere or globe much larger than any of Jupiter's satellites. It appeared to stand out in space between the planet and the observer, was well and sharply defined, and most intensely black. It reflected no light, and was not seen either before or after its passage across the planet. It could not have been a spot on the globe of Jupiter, for it passed over its disc from first internal contact to last eternal contact of margins in three hours and nineteen minutes. It was not a satellite nor the shadow of one, because all the four satellites were in full view the whole time. It will be interesting to know whether other observers witnessed this curious transit.

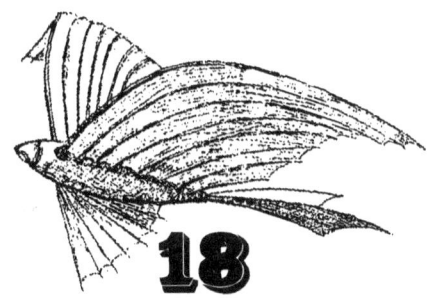

18
MOTHERSHIP OVER NEW JERSEY

April 12 - 13, 1879
Jersey City, New Jersey

ON THE NIGHT OF April 12, 1879, astronomer Henry Harrison, a member of the Toronto Astronomical Society, was at home on his telescope, searching the sky for Brorsen's Comet [5D/Brorsen], when he discovered something entirely different. In a letter published on April 17 in the *New York Tribune*, Harrison said, "At about 8:30 o'clock last evening, as I was searching for Brorsen's comet, I suddenly hit upon an object which I supposed to be a planetary nebula, very much resembling that near Beta Ursae Majoris [referring to the spherical nebula M97]."

THE REAL COWBOYS & ALIENS

M97 (NGC 3587), planetary nebula in Ursa Major--Göran Nilsson & The Liverpool Telescope [CC BY-SA 4.0 (https://creativecommons.org/licenses/by-sa/4.0)]

Astronomer and UFO researcher Morris K. Jessup (1900-1959) in his 1955 book *The Case for the UFO* states that Harrison's description of the object confirms it was an unidentified object under intelligent control and not a celestial body. "A planetary nebula is almost circular, and certainly not flat on one side. This object looked organic. We are vaguely reminded of some of the shapes of pyramids, bells, pears, etc., which have been reported for generations. Clearly a nebulous or gaseous object, freely suspended in space, would assume a symmetrical shape and fuzzy edges. This thing did neither. Its appearance alone indicates that it was a UFO. Its motion clinches the argument."

Harrison observed that the object maintained "not only its shape, diameter, and density, but also its luminosity" throughout the six hours that he viewed it, although it changed position several times and exhibited very fast movement. It was moving rapidly from the northwest to the southeast.

Original Article in New York Tribune, April 17, 1879

When he first spotted the strange luminous object at 8:30 p.m., it was located between the Pleiades and the variable star Algol. Leaving the telescope to check his charts to see what celestial object was supposed to be in that position, he found none. When he returned to his telescope, the UFO had moved out of the field of view where he had previously seen it. Re-acquiring it with his telescope he found that it had moved four minutes in astronomical terms, which was much faster than a comet would move.

Thirty minutes later, the object had again moved four minutes. Harrison called a friend to come observe with him, and both men continued to track the strange object. Harrison later said, "A comet it could not be, because of its rapid motion from N.W. to S.E., nor could it have been a cloud..."

Researcher Cheryl Costa, writing about the incident for *SyracuseNewTimes.com*, said, "The object gave the appearance of hovering at a very high altitude, but Harrison realized that an object would have to be moving at great speed in order to remain overhead as the Earth turned. Needless to say, this mystified Harrison as he made his remarkable observations because, like it or not, the object was generally stationary [relative to the Earth] even as the stars rose and set behind it."

At this point, Harrison realized that he had to "obtain more knowledge about this wonderful phenomenon," and he decided to send a telegram at once to the Naval Observatory in Washington, D.C., hoping that they would track it and give him more information about it. Before leaving to send the telegram, he noticed that the object was rapidly approaching Alpha Gemini [Castor]. As it turned out, sending the telegram would prove fruitless, as the Naval Observatory staff ignored his report.

After returning from the telegraph office, Harrison continued tracking the object with his telescope and noted that "onward it moved with independent motion." At 2:10 a.m. on April 13, the object had moved to the zenith and "now seemed to be more brilliant than at any previous observation." He added, "I fancied I could see it with the unaided eye but cannot be positive of this."

OLD WEST UFOS: 1865-1895

"Considered from ANY approach, this object appears to have been organic, intelligently operated and hovering over New York City!" Morris K. Jessup wrote in his book *The Case for the UFO*. He explained, "Harrison's bell-shaped object was moving almost three times as fast as rotation of the earth would cause it to do. At first one hesitates to say that it was hovering, but a little mathematical deduction indicates an object merely drifting with currents of the upper air and at one hundred miles latitude would need to have but 2.4 miles per hour velocity over the ground, and at ten miles above New York and appearing in Dec. 37° north, it would be drifting only a quarter mile per hour and would have been but seven-tenths of a mile south of Harrison's observing point and therefore directly over New York Harbor. Furthermore, if the object was actually moving in a straight line, overhead, it would appear to speed up slightly when it crossed his meridian (the NS line) and this is precisely what it did. And, assuming that it shifted its position slightly so as to pass nearly over the city, its shift of a little more than half a degree of declination would indicate height of from ten to one hundred miles."

Researcher Cheryl Costa added, "Morris K. Jessup, using a combination of measurements from ... regional astronomers, calculated that the object was over New York City for three hours. He further determined that the object was at an altitude of 80 to 100 miles above the Earth and estimated the bell-shaped object to be about a half mile in diameter."

THE REAL COWBOYS & ALIENS

Although initially criticized by other astronomers for supposedly having mistaken Brorsen's Comet for the mystery object, later three astronomers stepped up and validated his observations about the object, including J. Spencer Devoe of Manhattan, who wrote a letter to the *New York Tribune* the same day that Harrison's observation appeared in the newspaper. Supporting what Harrison saw, Devoe wrote, "In today's issue of *The Tribune*, I saw a letter from Mr. Harrison describing a phenomenon seen by him on Saturday evening, resembling a moving nebula about the size of that near Beta Ursa Majoris, direction N.W. to S.E.... I had a similar experience; a bright luminous nebula-like object, which I could plainly see with the naked eye..."

New-York Tribune – April 26, 1879, Page 2

OLD WEST UFOS: 1865-1895

Additional support came from two other astronomers, Henry M. Parkhurst (1825-1908), who also wrote a letter confirming what Harrison saw, and many years later from Morris K. Jessup who said, "Whatever this thing was, and whatever may be the accuracy of our speculations as to its speed, distance and size, it exhibited motion inexplicable except as intelligent control."

In addition to the publication of Harrison's letter in the *New York Tribune*, it was also reproduced in the *Scientific American,* May 10, 1879, which was quite an accomplishment, given the strictly conservative nature of that latter publication. "It is to the everlasting credit of the very conservative editors that they could and did recognize this item, partially at least, for its true worth," Jessup wrote.

> [MAY 10, 1879.
>
> **A Curious Astronomical Phenomenon.**
>
> Under the date of April 13, Mr. Henry Harrison, of Jersey City, sends to the New York *Tribune* the following communication:
>
> "At about 8:30 o'clock last evening, as I was searching for Brorsen's comet, I suddenly hit upon an object which I supposed to be a planetary nebula, very much resembling that near Beta Ursa Majoris, nearly on a line north, between the Pleiades and the variable star Algol. Being somewhat in doubt as to the existence of such a nebula in that region, I started the driving clock, noted the right ascension and declination, which were 2h. 34m. and 37° N., searched the catalogues, but found no such object recorded. By this time I found the object gone out of the field, but soon found it again, when it had gained four min. in R. A., its declination being unchanged. A half hour or so later, watching it constantly with amazement, I found it had gained the same amount. I no longer trusted to my own vision, but called a friend to confirm what undoubtedly was there. He saw it, and we both began to speculate as to its physical composition. A comet it could not be, because of its rapid motion from N. W. to S. E., nor could it have been a cloud, because it maintained not only its shape, diameter and density, but also its luminosity, and in the absence of both sun and moon a batch of cloud viewed with a telescope would have no definition, form, or illumination. Still following it as it slowly swept toward Alpha Auriga, I found that a calculation of R. A. at 9:35 was 3h. 4m., N. D. 37°.

Portion of Article from Scientific American,
May 10, 1879

THE MISSING BALLOON.

Prof. Wise and his Companion Believed to have been Lost in Lake Michigan.

CHICAGO, Oct. 10.—The statement that a balloon was seen yesterday at Albion, Mich., is discredited here. It was claimed that the air ship was moving over that place in a southwesterly direction at a rapid pace. Telegrams to all towns lying southwest of Albion, beginning at South Bend, Ind., and ending at Bloomington, Ill., brought responses in each case that no balloon had been seen at any of them. There has been no ascension in this part of the United States since the Wise party started, and the claim of the Albion man, who reported that a balloon was visible there, is consequently doubted. It is believed that the last seen of Wise was by the railroad employees at Miller's Station, Ind., at midnight, thirty hours after the departure from St. Louis, as THE SUN has been already informed. The wind was then blowing a gale from the southwest, and the balloon, if it ever passed over Lake Michigan, toward which it was rapidly drifting, which is doubtful, must have gone to the vast wildernesses of Michigan, or perhaps to Canada. The absence of news concerning the missing balloon and its occupants, however, is accepted here as conclusive evidence that they must have gone down in Lake Michigan. If they had struck land anywhere this side of the Georgian Bay country they would have been discovered before this. They might have been lost in Lake Michigan without coming to the surface or being discovered, as Donaldson and his balloon have never been found, although it is certain that he perished in the lake.

The Sun, 10-11-1879, p.1

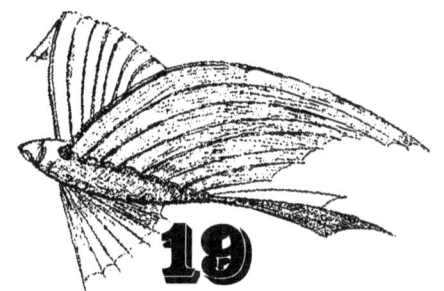

19
MYSTERIOUS AIRSHIP OVER IOWA

October 10, 1879
Dubuque, Iowa

BEFORE WE FULLY delve into the subject of this chapter, the sighting of a UFO over Iowa, it is beneficial to first look briefly into the career of ballooning pioneer John Wise (1808-1879). Wise was an early enthusiast in the field of ballooning, making over 400 balloon flights in his lifetime. At the age of 27, he made his first flight in a homemade balloon in Philadelphia on May 2, 1835. His ascent was unexciting but generally successful. His next few flights were semi-disastrous, but as the years went on his skills improved, until he emerged as one of the leading experts in the field.

In 1859, Wise attempted to make the first official "air mail" delivery in the United States, taking off in a balloon from Lafayette, Indiana, headed to New York. Weather issues forced him to land in Crawfordsville, Indiana, and the mail had to be sent on by train.

Professor John Wise

OLD WEST UFOS: 1865-1895

John Wise Uses a Balloon for First "Air Mail" Delivery in 1859

Eventually, Wise came up with several useful innovations in balloon safety. Then, on September 28, 1879, Wise embarked on his final mission aboard an airship called the *Pathfinder*.

Several days later, on the morning of October 10, 1879, a large, mysterious airship was seen moving over the city of Dubuque, Iowa, at a very high altitude. Although many people described it as a "balloon," that identification was based on an assumption that was later proven to be false. Many assumed that the "balloon" was Professor Wise's *Pathfinder* which had departed from Missouri on September 28 as stated earlier. Nobody knew it yet, but the *Pathfinder* had fallen into Lake Michigan just hours after it took off, killing Wise's assistant and presumably also Wise, although his body was never found.

THE REAL COWBOYS & ALIENS

Since this "mystery airship" seen over Dubuque does not seem to have been the *Pathfinder*, then what was it? This is a fascinating question that bears closer examination.

"People who were up at a very early hour this morning were astonished at seeing what appeared to be a large balloon going over the city. It was seen by quite a number of persons in different parts of the city and was visible for an hour."

The object was visible to the citizens below for an entire hour, meandering slowly to the south before finally disappearing to the southwest. Witnesses said it looked like a large balloon with a "car" attached, but no persons could be seen in the car.

One eyewitness, Thomas Lloyd, who worked for the local newspaper, later reported that he watched the airship for over an hour. It rose and fell as it moved along its course. Many other people also claimed to have seen the phenomenon.

The passing of the strange craft over Dubuque was reported in many regional newspapers of the day, including the *Fort Scott (Kansas) Daily Monitor*, the *Burlington (Vermont) Free Press*, the *Lawrence (Kansas) Daily Journal*, the *Muscatine (Iowa) Weekly Journal*, and many others.

Interestingly, an object of almost the exact same description had passed over the city of Albion, Michigan, one day earlier (October 9). As was the case in Dubuque, the citizenry assumed that it was Professor Wise's balloon, the *Pathfinder*, which had been reported missing but whose crash had not yet been confirmed.

THE BALLOON AGAIN.

An Air Ship Seen High in the Air by a Number of People at Dubuque Yesterday Morning.

[Special Telegram to The Inter Ocean.]

DUBUQUE, Iowa, Oct. 10.—People who were up at a very early hour this morning were astonished at seeing what appeared to be a large balloon going over the city. It was seen by quite a number of persons in different parts of the city, and was visible for an hour. It was at a great height, and appeared to have a car attached. It finally disappeared on the horizon, movin a southwesterly direction. There is much speculation as to what the mysterious stranger could have been.

[To the Western Associated Press.]

DUBUQUE, Iowa, Oct. 10.—Thomas Lloyd, a compositor on the *Times*, saw a balloon early this morning. He watched it for over an hour, and called the attentention of the telegraph operator to it. It was up very high, and the car could be seen, but no person. It was seen in the southeast, and traveled south slowly, rising and falling in its course. Numbers of others also claim they saw the air ship.

The Inter Ocean (Chicago, Ill.), 10-11-1879, p. 4

Albion, Michigan, is 371 miles due east of Dubuque. The balloon sighted there at 9 a.m. on October 9 was said to be "going southwest rapidly, at a great height." It also seemed to have a "car" attached. If it adjusted its course to more west than south, it could conceivably have flown over

Dubuque a day later. Therefore, it could have been the same object.

> **THE MISSING BALLOON.**
>
> ALBION, Mich., Oct. 9.—A large balloon passed over this city at 9 o'clock this morning, going southwest rapidly, at a great height. To all appearances a car was attached.

The Muscatine (Iowa) Journal, 10-9-1879, p. 1

Some people still believed that the Albion sighting and the Dubuque sighting were both of the *Pathfinder*, despite the fact that it was later estimated that Professor Wise's balloon had plunged into Lake Michigan either on September 28 or 29, killing both men on board.

A theory arose that after the *Pathfinder* fell into the lake, spilling out its human cargo, the balloon had risen back up into the sky and hence was seen over Albion and Dubuque. Eventually, the proponents of the theory said, it fell again into Lake Michigan, where the wreckage was discovered on October 10. Although it seems stranger than fiction to believe that the *Pathfinder* would crash twice in the same location after floating around freely for over a week, such was the theory proposed in an effort to explain the "mystery balloon" sightings over Albion and Dubuque.

The New York Sun went on record on Oct. 10 as disbelieving the idea that the *Pathfinder* could have been seen over Albion. From Albion, the balloon supposedly went to the southwest, but other towns located to the southwest of Albion reported that they saw no balloon. It's important to note, however, that if the object corrected its course shortly after leaving Albion and headed due east, then its appearance a day later in Dubuque can be defended.

It seems that the mystery of the 1879 airship must remain firmly in the category of "unsolved," since the *Pathfinder* explanation does not seem to hold water. No other airships were known to have been aloft on October 9 and 10, 1879, and therefore, what many people saw that day remains an enigma even all these years later.

MYSTERY IN THE SKY.

What was Seen at a New Mexican Railway Station.

SANTA FE, N. M., March 31.—A special to the *New Mexican*, from Galisteo Junction, has the following:

To-night, soon after the arrival of the train from Santa Fe, as the operator at this point and two or three friends were taking a short walk before retiring for the night, they were startled by voices evidently coming from above them. At first they supposed it was from some persons on the mountain near here, known as the Sierra Colorado, but on looking upwards they were astonished to see a large balloon coming from the west. As it rapidly approached the voices became more distinct, but were entirely unintelligible. Loud shouts, in a language entirely unknown to any of the party, were constantly given, evidently with a desire to attract attention.

The construction of the balloon was entirely different from anything of the kind ever seen by any of the party, being in the shape of a fish, and at one time was so low that fanciful characters on the outside of the car, which appeared to be very elegant, were plainly seen. The air machine appeared to be entirely under the control of the occupants, and to be guided by a large fan-like apparatus.

The party seemed to be enjoying themselves, as laughter and occasionally strains of music were heard.

A few articles were dropped from the car as the balloon passed over the junction, but owing to the imperfect light the only thing which was found was a magnificent flower, with a slip of exceedingly fine silk like paper, on which were some characters strongly resembling those on Japanese tea chests. One article which from its weight when thrown from the car, seemed to be a cup or some other piece of earthenware, could not be found to-night, but diligent search will be made for it in the morning. The balloon was monstrous in size, and the car, as near as could be judged, contained eight or ten persons. Another peculiar feature of the air machine was that the occupants could evidently sail at any height they choose, as soon after passing the junction, it assumed a great height and moved off very rapidly toward the east.

The cup thrown from the balloon is of very peculiar workmanship, entirely different from anything used in this country. Both flower and cup are in possession of the operator at the junction, and can be seen by any one who desires to see them.

This evening a collector of curiosities passed through this place, and on being shown the magnificent flower and cup dropped from the balloon which passed over this place last night, offered such a sum of money for them that it could not be refused, and he became the possessor of them. He gives it as his opinion that the balloon must have come from Asia, and thinks it possible it came from Jeddo.

The Tennessean, 4-3-1880, p.3

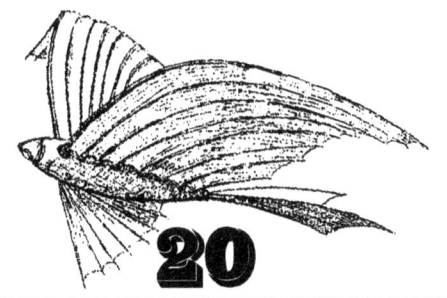

20
NEW MEXICO'S FIRST UFO
March 26, 1880
Galisteo, New Mexico

THROUGHOUT THE WORLD, the city of Roswell, New Mexico, is synonymous with unidentified flying objects, given the reported crash of a flying saucer at a remote ranch located north of Roswell in 1947. Interestingly though, there was another significant "UFO" encounter 67 years before the Roswell incident, at a town called Galisteo, New Mexico, about 100 miles north of where the Roswell crash is said to have occurred. The Galisteo event, which took place on March 26, 1880, is interesting enough that if the circumstances had been right and proper marketing had been done, the streets of Galisteo today could be lined with shops selling UFO and alien paraphernalia, as happened in Roswell. Delving into what occurred in Galisteo, we see some of the same elements that came to pass about a hundred years later, when the story about Roswell first broke in the 1980s.

Authors Noe Torres (left) and John LeMay (right) at the Roswell UFO Crash Site in 2012

Although the object that was observed in 1880 is sometimes described as an "airship" or "balloon," the sighting happened seventeen years before the "airship" craze that swept America in 1897, when hundreds of reports about mysterious airships came in from all over the United States. Also, the first untethered, steerable balloons, powered by internal combustion engines, did not take flight until 1898, nearly twenty years after this sighting.

OLD WEST UFOS: 1865-1895

The story first appeared in *The Santa Fe New Mexican* on Sunday, March 28, 1880, and it was published in newspapers as far away as Nashville, Tennessee. These written accounts told the story of an extraordinary event that happened 25 miles south of Santa Fe, in Galisteo, two days earlier, on March 26. The headlines read, "GALISTEO'S APPARITION - A mysterious Aerial Phantom appears at the Junction - A balloon becomes mysteriously visible overhead, and after a short stay departs for the east. From Asia probably."

Airship Design, 1896

According to the article, "shortly after the arrival of the train from Santa Fe," the operator of the train station and two or three of his friends were taking a short walk before retiring for the night, when they heard very unusual noises, including strange voices, coming from above them. Thinking the sounds were coming from a nearby mountain, known as the Sierra Colorada, the men lifted their gaze toward the mountain, and as they did so, they saw a "monstrous air machine" coming toward them from the west.

The Story Appeared in the Daily New Mexican, 3-28-1880

To the witnesses, the ship appeared to consist of two parts – an upper cylinder that they called "the balloon," and the lower passenger compartment that they referred to as "the car." The language they applied to their sighting was, understandably, the terminology associated with the parts of a typical air balloon of their time period. Since no other kinds of airborne vehicles existed in 1880, their use of vocabulary associated with balloons was logical. However, it is important to remember that in 1880, no balloons existed that could travel long distances with such speed and maneuverability.

The article continues, "The construction of the balloon was entirely different to anything of the kind ever seen by any of the party being in the shape of a fish, and at one time was so low that fanciful characters [written or printed characters] on the outside of the car which appeared to be very elegant were plainly seen. The air machine appeared to be entirely under the control of the occupants and appeared to be guided by a large fan like apparatus."

Continuing their description of the ship, the article says, "The balloon was monstrous in size, and the car as near as could be judged contained 8 or 10 persons. Another peculiar feature of the air machine was that the occupants could evidently sail at any height they choose, as soon after passing the junction, it assumed a great height and moved off very rapidly toward the east."

As the witnesses watched the airship move "rapidly" closer, the voices they had heard earlier became more distinct, and they began hearing what sounded like persons shouting very loudly to attract the attention of others. "The party seemed to be enjoying themselves as laughter and occasionally screams of mirth were heard." But, the strange thing about what they heard was that the language was totally unknown to any of the eyewitnesses.

As the airship passed over the men and across the small town of Galisteo, several objects fell out of it or were thrown to the ground below. One of the fallen objects was "a magnificent flower with a slip of exceedingly fine silk like paper, on which were some characters strongly resembling those on Japanese tea chests."

Another item that fell from the sky was a cup "of very peculiar workmanship, entirely different to anything used in this country." The cup, along with the flower, were kept by the train station operator who intended to put them on display for anyone who desired to see them.

THE REAL COWBOYS & ALIENS

Typical Japanese Tea Chests of the 19ᵗʰ Century

However, on the following evening (March 27), a passing "collector of curiosities" noticed the display of artifacts that fell from the airship and "offered such a sum of money for them that it could not be refused, and he became the possessor of them." In taking ownership of the two items, the proud collector gave his opinion that the airship must have come from Asia or Japan, presumably because of the foreign looking characters written on the silk paper found along with the flower.

Thus came to a close the strange episode of an airship that flew over Galisteo, New Mexico, on Friday, March 26, 1880, seventeen years before mysterious airships became a common sight all over the United States and 67 years before another airship crashed near Roswell, New Mexico, in what would become the world's best known UFO case.

What are some of the similarities between the two cases, one might ask? The first is geography, as they occurred within 100 miles of each other. The second is that strange artifacts were found in both cases and some of the artifacts contained a strange writing (characters) that nobody could decipher. Third, the artifacts recovered both at Roswell and in Galisteo were taken away and never seen again. Fourth, both the Galisteo object and the Roswell UFO were generally moving from west to east when they were spotted. And, fifth, the construction of both objects was described as "entirely different to anything of the kind ever seen."

Traveling Curio Collector, Circa 1900 (Wikimedia)

So clearly, Galisteo's UFO incident was New Mexico's first big brush with the whole milieu of UFOs and aliens that later came to define the state so dramatically after the Roswell UFO crash of 1947. It started in Galisteo, and if the town had played its cards right, the state's big UFO museum might have been established there, instead of 200 miles to the south, in Roswell.

THE REAL COWBOYS & ALIENS

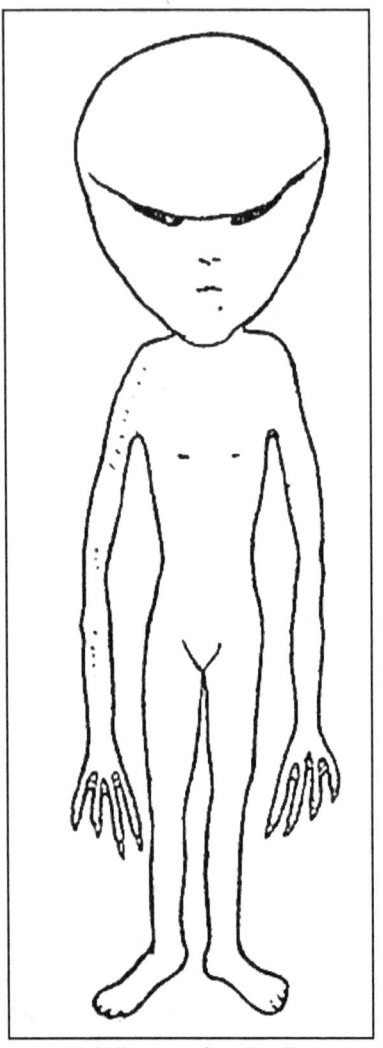

Drawing of Grey Alien by Leonard H. Stringfield. Courtesy Dell Stringfield/Stringfield Estate

21
ALIENS ON THE BRIDGE
April 1880
Cameron Mills, New York

OUR NEXT STORY differs from many in this book not because of its content, but because of its source. Rather than a period newspaper article, this story was kept as a secret for four generations within the family of the key witnesses involved. Ufologist Cheryl Costa interviewed the 80-year-old great-grandniece of three of the witnesses, who told her the story. "They had passed the story down from generation to generation, almost as a family heirloom," Costa told us when we interviewed her for this chapter.

The incident took place near Cameron Mills, New York [today simply Cameron]. On an April afternoon in 1880, two sisters named Elizabeth and Eva were walking to their town's one-room schoolhouse. They were accompanied by several other children as well. Upon approaching a small bridge crossing over a stream, they noticed something strange on the other side. All along the embankment of the creek near the opposite end of the bridge were a group of what the children simply called "little people." These "little people" motioned for the children to come across the bridge. But, because their parents had cautioned the children to be wary of strangers, they turned around and ran back home.

Typical One-Room Schoolhouse of the Period

The most interesting part of this story is the description given by the children of the strange "little people," stating that they were "small, skinny, and oddly colored" -- "oddly colored" in this case meaning grey. Furthermore, they were bald and had big eyes. As for attire, they were said to wear something resembling blue coveralls. Some recent online posts claim the beings wore skintight, shiny metallic looking suits, but no such description was given in the original story.

OLD WEST UFOS: 1865-1895

And the final disturbing detail: long spindly fingers. Essentially, these 1880 school children gave a perfect description of the grey aliens which did not enter the public consciousness until nearly 100 years later. The fact that creatures looking exactly like grey aliens were seen in 1880 is a staggeringly unexpected disclosure. Most people assume that grey aliens were unknown until the 1960s.

Steuben County, in the area near Cameron Mills

UFO researcher Cheryl Costa first obtained the story in 2014 from an elderly relative of the two sisters and their brother. Costa told us, "I was invited to a backyard barbecue by acquaintances. During the introductions, the hostess told her visiting relatives that I was a journalist and wrote a column for the *Syracuse New Times* about UFOs. That drew the usual chatter and many rounds of questions that I frequently get. Later at the event, a woman in her 80s took me aside with another relative and shared the 1880 story. They showed me a very old photo album and a 'tintype' photo of the two great-grand aunts together as young adults. The aunts were two of the young children in the [UFO] event. They made it clear they wanted family anonymity."

Costa also told us, "After several of these invitations to backyard picnics and some dinner parties, I came to the conclusion that some families are handing UFO stories down like family heirlooms. I always left one of these events with one or two personal accounts with details in my reporter's notebook. Some of the accounts I was able to publish on condition of anonymity; others I chose not to publish because the account circumstances would 'out' the observer/experiencer."

Costa told the authors of this book that she is "absolutely convinced" that the story is true. Respecting the family's wishes, Costa will not disclose the identity of the witnesses involved in the 1880 event. "Ever since I wrote that article, I've had several upstate New York historians ask – no, beg me -- to identify one or more of the families in Cameron Mills. I consulted with the family who shared with me, and they specifically asked me to protect the family's identity. As a reporter, I protect my sources."

Although we were able to find no contemporaneous accounts of this remarkable incident, the research that has been conducted by Costa, who is considered one of the most thorough and highly-reputable UFO researchers of our current era, is extremely compelling. Hopefully more details will come to light regarding this fascinating account one day, but for now it remains an amazing 19th century close encounter of the third kind.

Spring-Heeled Jack, a fiendish figure from 1830's England

22
SPRING HEELED JACK IN KENTUCKY?

July 1880
Louisville, Kentucky

IN JULY 1880, a strange, madly leaping humanoid literally sprang onto the scene, terrifying citizens in and around Louisville, Kentucky, according to numerous sources including Jeffrey Scott Holland, author of *Weird Kentucky*. The mysterious figure was tall and thin; wore a jumpsuit and helmet; and had a lamp on his chest. He was capable of leaping incredibly high into the air and was reported to have jumped entirely over a horse-drawn carriage and also over a haystack. In the process of jumping around and scaring people, the creature was occasionally known to grab and rip at women's clothing. According to the web site *StrangeHistory.org*: "...women in Louisville, Kentucky began to report that they had been attacked by a man-like creature wearing black, tight clothing and a cape. He could jump great heights and distances. The attacker had long pointed fingers, ears and nose and would spit a blue glowing flame...."

Period Illustration of Spring-Heeled Jack

This unearthly creature drew comparisons to the entity that terrorized parts of London, England, in the 1830s, known as Spring-Heeled Jack. In the London sightings, the creature had exhibited much of the same behavior as in Kentucky. It would leap vast distances, sometimes seemed to be carrying a lamp on its chest, occasionally ripped at women's clothing, was described as terrifying, and generally caused panic and alarm among the populace. Witnesses to the London sightings also claimed the humanoid shot out blue flames and had metallic claws for hands. Considering these descriptions, the creature was obviously not a human and, some would argue, might have been an extraterrestrial. That point was driven home by researcher Phil Rife in *Fate* magazine, who asked, "Is this legendary leaper an agile lunatic or energetic alien?"

> Actually, he'd paid a brief visit to U.S. as early as 1880. In July of that year, someone in Louisville, Kentucky, was practicing Jack's favorite trick of accosting women and tearing at their clothing. The attacker — who was described as tall, with pointed ears, a long nose, and long fingers — wore a cape, shiny uniform, and helmet. He's said to have sported on his chest a bright light which spouted a blue flame at his victims. He made his escapes in typical Jack fashion by jumping effortlessly over obstacles like wagons and haystacks in a single bound.

Rife, Phil. "Springheel Jack Invades America." Fate Magazine, November 1997, p.17

As Rife points out, there were reported sightings of this jumping humanoid around Louisville in July 1880, which is especially interesting in view of two documented UFO sightings in the area that same month! On Thursday, July 29, 1880, the *Louisville Courier-Journal* reported the first of two very strange UFO incidents that could possibly have been related to the humanoid sightings.

The article "A Flying Machine" disclosed an incident that happened the day before, Wednesday, July 28, in which a strange "man" was seen piloting an even stranger flying machine. The article says, "Between 6 and 7 o'clock last evening while C.A. Youngman and Ben Floxner were standing at a side window of Haddart's drugstore" the men saw "an object high up in the air" hovering over the Ohio River Bridge. At first the men thought it was merely the wreck of a toy balloon. But, as it got closer they observed that it "had the appearance of a man surrounded by machinery, which he seemed to be working with his feet and hands."

Though the witnesses didn't really describe the man within the sphere, it seems too much a coincidence that the sphere showed up around the same time as the mysterious jumping humanoid. As for the craft itself, it sounded a bit like an autogyro, a relatively small helicopter-like craft that wasn't invented until 50 years later.

Autogyro

OLD WEST UFOS: 1865-1895

The article says that the mysterious pilot "worked his feet as though he was running a treadle," which was a mechanism activated by a foot pedal on old sewing machines. The article said that the man's arms seemed to be "swinging to and fro above his head, though the latter movement sometimes appeared to be executed with wings or fans." The mention of wings is interesting, because Spring-Heeled Jack was occasionally described as having wings. Naturally, the witnesses to this flying man were greatly excited, becoming "considerably worked up by the apparition, and inspected it very closely."

From here we get some more good descriptions of the craft: "[The witnesses] could see the delicate outlines of machinery, but the object was too high up to make out its exact construction. At times it would seem to be descending, and then the man appeared to exert himself considerably, and ran the machine faster, when it would ascend again and assume a horizontal position. It did not travel as fast as a paper balloon, and its course seemed to be entirely under the control of the aeronaut. At first it was traveling in a southeastward direction, but when it reached a point just over the city, it turned and went due south, until it had passed nearly over the city, when it taxed to the southwest, in which direction it was going when it passed out of sight in the twilight of the evening."

"The gentlemen who saw it are confident that it was a man navigating the air on a flying machine. His movements were regular, and the machine was under the most perfect control. If he belongs to this mundane sphere he should have dropped his card as he passed over, to enlighten those who saw him, and that his friends, if he has any, might be informed of his whereabouts."

> **A FLYING MACHINE.**
>
> WHAT TWO LOUISVILLIANS SAW LAST EVENING.
>
> Between 6 and 7 o'clock last evening while Messrs. C. A. Youngman and Ben Flexner were standing at a side window of Haddart's drug store, at Second and Chestnut streets, looking skyward, they discovered an object high up in the air apparently immediately above the Ohio river bridge, which they at first thought was the wreck of a toy balloon. As it got nearer they observed that it had the appearance of a man surrounded by machinery, which he seemed to be working with his feet and hands. He worked his feet as though he was running a treadle, and his arms seemed to be swinging to and fro above his head, though the latter movement sometimes appeared to be executed with wings or fans. The gazers became considerably worked up by the apparition, and inspected it very closely. They could see the delicate outlines of machinery, but the object was too high up to make out its exact construction.

The Courier-Journal (Louisville, Kentucky), 7-29-1880, p. 4

Only an hour or two later, a second sighting was recorded in Madisonville, Kentucky. A family observed a "circular form" that changed into an "oval." It also had "a ball at each end of the thing." In full, the relevant portions of the article, titled "The Flying Machine," are as follows: "Dr. DS

OLD WEST UFOS: 1865-1895

Dempsey, of Madisonville, Kentucky, has written the following to the *Madisonville Times* concerning the flying machine which was observed passing over the city two weeks ago:

The Courier-Journal, 8-6-1800, p.4

"I interviewed Mr. Wells, the proprietor of the marble shop, N. Main St., and Mr. Royster, a workman in said shop, in regard to what he and his family saw hop over Madisonville last Wednesday [July 28], but was not positive as to the day. Mr. Wells stated that Mr. Royster told him about it the day that an account of a flying machine over Louisville was published in the *Courier-Journal*. I asked them both, particularly Mr. Wells, was it before we received the *Courier-Journal*. This reply was emphatic, that it was in the morning of the day we received said *Courier-Journal*."

"Mr. Royster stated that the evening before, which would be Wednesday [July 28], between sundown and dark, his son Johnny, six or seven years old, called his attention to something he saw hopping over Madisonville. He, Mr. Royster, and his wife and other children went out and looked at it. They live in southeastern Madisonville, about half a mile from the railroad depot. He said there seem to be a ball at each end of the thing, and it looked as if it was about over the depot. It sometimes appeared in a circular form and changed into an oval. It passed out of sight going, as well as he could determine, directly south. Everybody knows Mr. Wells and will believe that what he said in regard to the time Mr. Royster told him these things is strictly true."

Perhaps the leaping and flying humanoid was not happy with the performance of his flying machine, because several weeks later, a figure resembling him was seen over New York City, flying only with the aid of "wings" and "frog legs." An article in the *New York Times* on September 12, 1880, stated, "One day last week, a marvelous apparition was seen near Coney Island. At the height of at least a thousand feet in the air a strange object was in the act of flying toward the New Jersey coast. It was apparently a man with bat's wings and improved frog's legs. The face of the man could be distinctly seen, and it wore a cruel and determined expression."

The article goes on to mention that a similar sight had been seen several weeks prior in both Kentucky and in St. Louis, Missouri.

OLD WEST UFOS: 1865-1895

> **AN AERIAL MYSTERY.**
>
> One day last week a marvelous apparition was seen near Coney Island. At the height of at least a thousand feet in the air a strange object was in the act of flying toward the New-Jersey coast. It was apparently a man with bat's wings and improved frog's legs. The face of the man could be distinctly seen, and it wore a cruel and determined expression. The movements made by the object closely resembled those of a frog in the act of swimming with his hind legs and flying with his front legs. Of course, no respectable frog has ever been known to conduct himself in precisely that way; but were a frog to wear bat's wings, and to attempt to swim and fly at the same time, he would correctly imitate the conduct of the Coney Island monster. When we add that this monster waved his wings in answer to the whistle of a locomotive, and was of a deep black color, the alarming nature of the apparition can be imagined. The object was seen by many reputable persons, and they all agree that it was a man engaged in flying toward New-Jersey.
>
> About a month ago an object of precisely the same nature was seen in the air over St. Louis by a number of citizens who happened to be sober and are believed to be trustworthy. A little later it was seen by various Kentucky persons as it flew across the State. In no instance has it been known to alight, and no one has seen it at a lower elevation than a thousand feet above the surface of the earth. It is without doubt the most extraordinary and wonderful object that has ever been seen, and there should be no time lost in ascertaining its precise nature, habits, and probable mission.

The New York Times, 9-12-1880, p.6

Was it coincidental that at the same time that the amazing, high-jumping humanoid was seen around Louisville, there were also two sightings of a strange UFO buzzing around in the skies above, with possibly related sightings in St. Louis and New York City a short time later?

Sightings of these leaping humanoids had apparently occurred around the country prior to 1880. During the Civil War on the battlefield of Gettysburg, Pennsylvania, in July of 1863 was seen a strange "Spring-Heeled" being 'flittering' around the dead. The man-thing was described as being tall with glowing green eyes and wearing a dark cape or cloak of some kind.

Furthermore, 1880 wasn't the last time this phenomenon was seen in America. In May of 1905 the jumping humanoid came to Philadelphia, Pennsylvania. A woman named Julia McGlone was leaving work when a figure leapt down and attacked her with sharp claws. The woman screamed, drawing the attention of a policeman who ran to her rescue. In the "Spring-Heeled Jack" tradition, the creature blew blue flames at the man's face and then jumped up a flight of stairs in a single bound! The strange being was wearing metallic looking clothing.

In more recent times, most UFO occupants that have been spotted by witnesses have not been quite as "jumpy" as in the 1800s. If the reader might forgive the pun, they seem to have lost the spring in their step.

23
MYSTERY LIGHTS OF MARFA, TEXAS

Circa 1883
Marfa, Texas

UFOs RARELY APPEAR on any sort of schedule, which makes spotting one extremely difficult. Usually, there is a lot of luck involved in seeing something out of the ordinary, the witness just happening to be at the right place at the right time. However, in West Texas, there is a strange phenomenon that may be UFO-related and has been happening almost every night since at least the 1800s, called "The Marfa Lights."

The lights are brightly glowing balls of fire that float and dance along the horizon every night beginning at around sundown. These "orbs" of light will suddenly sputter to life, like someone lighting a campfire. They will sparkle and grow brighter, float around, move left and right, move up and down, and then suddenly, will grow dim and go out.

Artist Neil Riebe's Conception of Marfa Lights

This apparition is hard to explain in words, but most people who actually see the lights are amazed and thrilled by them. That is why the State of Texas has built a special "Marfa Lights Viewing Area." The site has bathrooms and pay telescopes for viewing the lights. It is located on U.S. Highway 90, about nine miles east of Marfa, Texas. In order to see the lights, spectators look off to the southwest, toward the Chinati Mountains, and wait for the lights to appear every evening at around dusk, continuing long into the night.

On any given night, the Marfa Lights viewing area fills up with curious people hoping to catch a glimpse of these mysterious lights. Getting a good view of the lights often depends on the weather, cloud conditions, and so on. The lights seem more "active" on certain nights, and there seem to be more lights appearing on some nights than on others.

*Chinati Mountain Range Near Marfa, Texas
(Photo by Noe Torres)*

Some people have associated the mysterious lights with UFOs, and the locals have told of many UFO sightings that have been recorded in the Marfa area over the years. Probably the best known UFO story from this region is that of a reported mid-air collision between a small plane and a UFO in 1974. The incident, known as "Mexico's Roswell," occurred about 30 miles from where the Marfa Lights are seen.

For many years, scientists and skeptics alike have tried to explain away these puzzling lights as something normal. Some say they are headlights from cars traveling on a nearby highway. Other people say they are balls of gas or electrical energy. Still others say they are some form of geothermal energy that is escaping from the Earth's core. Some even speculate they are a previously unknown bioluminescent life form!

Photo of the Marfa Lights by Noe Torres

The first serious attempt to discover their mystery came in the late 1800s. A railroad engineer named Walter T. Harris used surveyor's methods to find the exact location of the strange lights, but he was not successful and concluded that the lights might be coming from deep within Mexico.

Over the decades, people have chased them. Airplanes have followed them. Scientists have studied them. Television programs have been done about them. Books have been written about them. And still, nobody knows for sure what they are. They remain one of Texas' most enduring and fascinating mysteries.

So, let's go back in time to one of the very first sightings ever recorded of the Marfa Lights. The year was 1883, and Texas was very much a dusty, frontier territory. The Southern Pacific Railway had just arrived at Marfa in January 1882, and the area was still mostly open range land with very few inhabitants.

OLD WEST UFOS: 1865-1895

A cowboy named Robert Reed Ellison and several other men had been herding cattle through the area around Marfa. On their second night in the area, they camped at a place called Paisano Pass. Suddenly, Ellison saw flickering lights in the distance and thought they were campfires lit by Apaches.

Cattle Roundup in Marfa, Texas Circa 1936

Scrambling onto their horses, Ellison and his men went out into the desert, looking for the source of the mysterious lights. For hours, the men searched along the base of the Chinati Mountains and in the mesa between their camp and where the lights had been. They saw no evidence that Apaches had been anywhere in the area. They found no tracks, no doused campfires, and no other clues. Ellison was extremely puzzled and began to think that the lights were something very unusual.

THE REAL COWBOYS & ALIENS

For the next two nights, Ellison and his men again saw the strange lights. They were never able to solve the mystery, though.

Later, Ellison talked to local residents about what he had seen. They told him that many local people saw the lights frequently. Sometimes, people would wander out into the desert trying to find the lights or evidence about the lights, such as ashes that indicated a campfire. But nobody had ever found any trace of what might cause the lights.

It seems likely that the lights were seen even before 1883. Historical accounts show that strange lights in the sky were seen by people riding on wagon trains from Ojinaga, Mexico, to San Antonio, Texas, back in the 1840s.

There is even a legend that says the lights are the ghost of a notorious Native American chief named Alsate, who lived in the mid-1800s. Alsate grew up in Mexico, across the Rio Grande River from Lajitas, Texas. He was of the Mescalero Apaches and became a powerful and greatly feared war chief of the tribe. Alsate and his warriors went on frequent raids into Mexico, which caused the government to hunt him down.

The Mexican authorities eventually captured Alsate, executed him near Presidio, Texas, and then scattered his remaining followers, selling them into slavery throughout Mexico. After the chief's death, stories were told about his ghost being seen in the mountainous areas around Marfa, Texas, where the tribe used to camp. According to this legend, the mysterious Marfa Lights are also part of Alsate's ghostly apparitions.

OLD WEST UFOS: 1865-1895

A Mescalero Apache Medicine Man, Circa 1880s

In part because of this legend, the nearby Chinati Mountains are called the Ghost Mountains, and the strange lights are often called the Marfa "ghost lights." This incredible story is just another part of the continuing mystery of the Marfa Lights.

Over the years, the legend of the lights remained of interest mostly to Texans, and occasional articles appeared in the state's newspapers and journals, such as a story titled "Ghost Light Appears in Marfa Area," published in the *San Angelo (Texas) Standard-Times* on Friday, February 9, 1945 (p. 13). The phenomenon remained mostly unknown outside the state of Texas until the first widely-circulated article about the lights was published in July 1957 in the national publication *Coronet*.

THE REAL COWBOYS & ALIENS

The Mystery of the Texas Ghost Light

by PAUL MORAN

FROM A small isolated peak in the Chinati Mountains some 18 miles from the Rio Grande, a mysterious light gleams out of the night like a weird Cyclopean eye. Settlers first reported it more than 70 years ago, and it still can be plainly seen from Highway 90 between Alpine and Marfa, Texas. Yet to this day, no one knows what it is, where it originates, or why it shines.

Uncounted numbers of "prospectors" have sought the ghost light's source. Approached from the air, or over the 50 miles of sun-seared terrain, it suddenly vanishes.

It is an intriguing sight, this strange light twinkling in the distance like a star resting on a mountain slope. Old natives will tell you that it is a campfire kindled by an ancient Apache ghost condemned to roam the mountains forever.

The light has a peculiar habit of moving. Viewed through a telescope, its faraway gleam will fade out only to return again a few degrees to the right or left. It is lighter in color than starlight and at times appears to be a double light. One minute it is a tiny, almost indistinct sparkle, the next a vivid glare brighter than an automobile headlight. At times, there is no light at all.

Perhaps the most popular theory explains it as a reflection of the moon from an undiscovered mica vein. But to allow a reflection to move, the vein would have to be a large, exposed lode which would have been discovered by now.

Luminous gas, such as the kind called "swamp gas," might be responsible for the light. But could it be seen 50 miles away? Furthermore, geologic conditions seem to discount the possibility of natural gas reserves there.

What about a mirage? Inverse mirages require a special type of stratified air that probably abounds in the Chinatis. But mirages are reflections of distant and, in this case, artificial lights. And 70 years ago the brightest light in this area was a kerosene lantern.

Other theories range from foxfire and uranium deposits to a cowboy's flashlight. Perhaps some day one of these will be the answer to the mystery. But up to now, no one knows.

JULY, 1957

Article in Coronet magazine, July 1957, p. 57

However, it was not until the late 1970s and early 1980s that the mysterious lights achieved a sort of "cult" status. The 1976 book *Tales of the Big Bend*, by Elton Miles, included stories about the lights dating to the 19th century and also contained a photograph of the Marfa Lights taken by a local rancher.

OLD WEST UFOS: 1865-1895

Following the publication of Miles' book, the Marfa Lights were featured on several national television shows in the 1980s and 1990s, including a wildly popular episode of the CBS series *Unsolved Mysteries*, airing on October 25, 1989. The lights were also examined on an episode of the Fox TV show *Sightings*, aired on September 25, 1992.

Photo of Alien near Marfa City Limits Sign (Brad Newton)

THE REAL COWBOYS & ALIENS

Artist Gustave Dore often Depicted Angels with Huge Swords, as in this Illustration from an 1866 Bible

24
THE SWORD FROM OUTER SPACE

1883
Ulster County, New York

IN 1912 Edgar Rice Burroughs published *A Princess of Mars* in *All-Story Magazine*. It was the first entry in what would become his "John Carter of Mars" series. The story saw Civil War era Confederate cavalryman John Carter being magically transported to Mars, called Barsoom by the local inhabitants. The series was different from most science fiction in that it was more fantasy based and included a great deal of sword play. Specifically, Carter was forced to fight in various gladiatorial arenas against different alien races and creatures. In fact, one of the later novels was even titled *Swords of Mars*.

Some people say that perhaps one of these "Swords of Mars" somehow fell out of the sky and crashed somewhere in Ulster County in New York State in 1883. The article "Born of a Ball of Fire" was published in the June 17th edition of the *New York Times*. Though the sword was quickly labeled a hoax by a local antiques dealer, we are left to wonder how the dealer would be qualified to judge whether it really was a sword from outer space.

Here are the facts of the case, or at least the "facts" according to the *Times*. Sometime around midnight, on April 17th of 1883, local physician T.O. Keator was riding along the bank of Rondout Creek when he experienced something remarkable. First, he heard a strange whirring noise and then witnessed a fireball about the size of a cartwheel strike the ground. In fact, the object touched down less than 40 feet away from him. Looking at the steaming remains on the ground, Keator wanted to get closer, but his spooked horse refused to get near it.

As usual, there is another version of the story, ever so slightly different, which has the fireball plunging into the river: "At about 2 o'clock on the morning of 17 April last Dr. Thomas O. Koater, of Accord, who is described as a man of excellent standing and unimpeachable veracity, was driving home after a visit to a patient. As he was going along the road by the Rondout River, a large ball of fire descended from the sky and buried itself in the river near the roadside, greatly startling Dr. Koater and his horse."

Unfortunately, the next morning when Keator informed the property owner Daniel D. Bell [also called by newspapers a "citizen of high standing"] about the incident, a search by Bell yielded nothing. And then on May 7th that same year, Bell's son, sixteen year old Raloy H. Bell, and a friend noticed something strange in the creek. An article in the June 23rd edition of the *Dunkirk Evening Observer* recapped the find: "...on 7 May a young son of Mr. Bell discovered under the water of the river at that spot which was only some four or five feet deep, the sword which has occasioned so much local excitement. The hilt was buried in the sand to the depth of about 2 feet, and the blade, projecting upward, was bent over nearly double. It was pulled up by a boat hook and was found to be covered with rust. The weapon was straightened and scoured by Mr. Bell, and has been inspected, free of charge, by great numbers of people from the surrounding country."

After the sword was straightened, Bell took it into town, where it caused a furor of excitement as people learned of its supposed celestial origin. The fact that the sword was possibly from space wasn't the only weird thing about it.

The original description said that the sword was made entirely of steel, weighed 17 pounds and had a double edged blade which was "not very sharp" and was "2 inches and three quarters wide at its broadest part, which is in the middle." The hilt was nearly 11 inches long, "furnishing grip for the hand of a giant in a fairytale, and is equipped with two guards, one being at right angles to the other."

"A few inches below it [the first guard] is an additional guard in the shape of a crosspiece." The article also said that the blade was "etched on both sides with some apparently meaningless figures and characters which may be intelligible however to the inhabitants of Mars or some other distant planet."

The article concluded by stating, "The people of Accord and its neighborhood are said to be firmly convinced of the celestial origin of the weapon and the reporter was assured that they would not receive with favor his suggestion that perhaps it had once belonged to the Cardiff giant [a 10-foot-tall gypsum statue of a giant that the owner in 1869 tried to pass off as an actual giant that had been 'petrified']."

The New York Times, 6-17-1883, p.10

That was the description given in the *Dunkirk Evening Observer's* version. The earlier article, "Born of a Ball of Fire" from the times on June 17th, described the sword as "covered with strange and puzzling hieroglyphics, which look as much as anything else like an outline drawing of the map of Greece. They are a succession of dots made by punching the metal with a sharp instrument. Some of the figures are labyrinthal in their character, and, like a wagon tire, seem to have no beginning nor ending. Others look like letters of the alphabet, with just enough dissimilarity to baffle their translation. Several have intricate geometric shapes, so mixed with meaningless lines as almost to destroy the outline."

These strange hieroglyphics are as fascinating as debris found in Corona, New Mexico, relating to the Roswell UFO crash of 1947, which was also said to have puzzling hieroglyphic writing on them. The sword's immense size was also intriguing considering that there are more than a few accounts of gigantic aliens in this book series, such as those that crashed in the Indian Ocean in the 1860s.

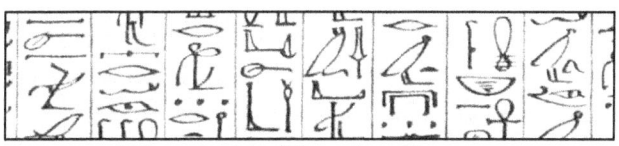

Hieroglyphics Found on Papyrus

The sword's strange origin and appearance fueled even more speculation: "[Ulster County residents] agree that [the sword] came down from some far-off planet, warped by the heat from its rapid journey through space and rusted by its short rest on the river bottom. It is believed, then, that some sanguinary giant had it wrested from its grasp and flung over the edge of his planetary residence, whence it whirled away through millions of miles of space on its trip to this little globe. Others think it might have been forged in one of the volcanic craters on the moon and fell through."

The article then concludes by stating that, "The fortunate owner has refused $1,000 for it, and one of his neighbors has offered to give his farm in exchange for the curiosity."

Eventually the *New York Times* brought in antiquities dealer Gaston L. Feuardent to examine the "space sword." In his opinion it was a poorly done "forgery." He stated that, "It has not one solitary point to indicate that it was not made in New York State within the past year."

And what should we make of Feuardent's assessment? Was he correct? Or, did he work for a late 18th century version of the Men in Black? Okay, that last part was wild conjecture, but how exactly would he know for certain that the sword didn't come from outer space? Whether the sword was "real" or not, Dr. Koater did see a great ball of fire crash in that exact spot. And, who in their right mind would make a sword that large, and for what purpose? As with most of the cases in this book, we may never know.

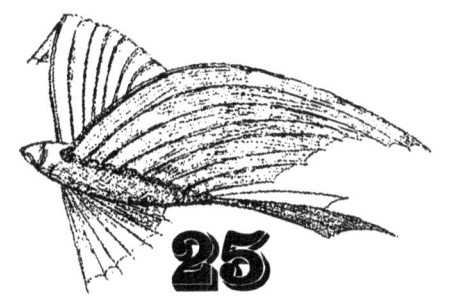

25
COWBOYS WITNESS UFO CRASH

June 6, 1884
Benkelman, Nebraska

IT'S A HOT SUMMER NIGHT on a remote ranch where a cowboy witnesses a strange UFO come crashing to the ground. No, we're not talking about rancher Mack Brazel and the Roswell, New Mexico, UFO crash. We're talking about an incident that predates Roswell by over 60 years!

On Friday, June 6, 1884, a very strange thing happened while John W. Ellis and three other cowboys were rounding up cattle on a remote ranch about 35 miles northwest of Benkelman, Nebraska. The cowboys said they saw a flying saucer crash in a nearby ravine. The incident was reported in two separate newspapers of that time, the *Nebraska Nugget* and the *Daily State Journal* of Lincoln, Nebraska. About the area where it happened, the *Nugget* reported, "The country in the vicinity is rather wild and rough, and the roads are hardly more than trails."

Artist's Conception of Event by Neil Riebe

The cattle roundup was suddenly interrupted when the three cowboys heard "a terrific whirring noise" in the sky above them. Looking up, they saw a blazing streak of light shooting down toward the ground. The witnesses later described it as a cylindrical airship, about 50 or 60 feet long and about 10 or 12 feet wide. It was composed of a strange metal that they later found to be extremely light.

OLD WEST UFOS: 1865-1895

The fiery cylinder struck the earth some distance away from where the cowboys stood. They could not see exactly where it had crashed, because it had fallen into a deep ravine.

The *Daily State Journal* later reported, "John W. Ellis, a well-known ranchman, was going out to his herd in company with three of his herders and several other cowboys engaged in the annual roundup. While riding along a draw they heard a terrific rushing, roaring sound overhead, and looking up, saw what appeared to be a blazing meteor of immense size falling at an angle to the earth. A moment later it struck the ground out of sight over the bank."

Ellis and the others turned their horses and set off in search of the crash site. Moments later, they found it. According to the *Nebraska Nugget*, the cowboys saw wreckage of a very strange appearance. The newspaper said, "He [Ellis] rode at once to the spot, and it is asserted, saw fragments of cog-wheels, and other pieces of machinery lying on the ground, scattered in the path made by the aerial visitor, glowing with heat so intense as to scorch the grass for a long distance around each fragment and made it impossible for one to approach it."

Although "cog-wheels" makes it sound like ordinary machinery, the witnesses may not have known how to describe it more exactly. They probably were just using images and words with which they were familiar.

More description was given about the wreckage: "One piece that looked like the blade of a propeller screw of a metal of an appearance like brass, about sixteen inches wide, three inches thick and three and a half feet long, was picked up by a spade. It would not weigh more than five pounds but appeared as strong and compact as any known metal. A fragment of a wheel with a milled rim, apparently having had a diameter of seven or eight feet, was also picked up. It seemed to be of the same material and had the same remarkable lightness."

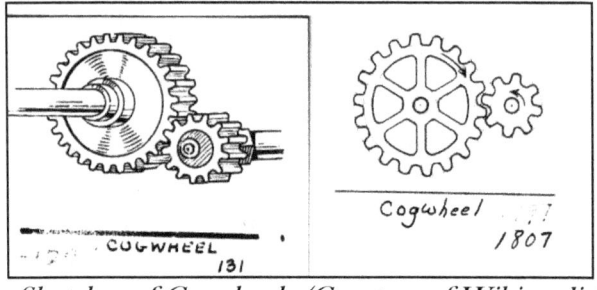

Sketches of Cogwheels (Courtesy of Wikimedia)

Interestingly, other reported UFO crashes that happened many decades later often included descriptions of extremely light metals. For example, in the 1947 Roswell UFO Crash, witnesses claimed to have seen pieces of a metal that was very light and flexible but also very strong.

After witnessing the crash, the three cowboys approached the still-burning object. "Coming to the edge of the deep ravine into which the strange object had fallen, they undertook to see what it was. But the heat was so great that the air about it was fairly ablaze and it emitted a light so dazzling that the eye could not rest upon it more than a moment."

One of the cowboys, whose name was given as Alf Williamson, dismounted and approached the crashed UFO. Closing to within 200 feet of the blazing wreckage, Williamson stuck his head over the edge of the ravine. Within 30 seconds, he "fell senseless from gazing at it at too close quarters." His hair was "singed to a crisp" and his face was covered with blisters.

The injured man was dragged away from the intensely hot area and taken to John W. Ellis' house, where he was cared for until a doctor could arrive to treat his wounds. His condition was said to be serious, and his brother, who lived in Denver, was summoned by telegraph.

This is one of the first accounts of a person being harmed during a UFO encounter. Although the injuries were described as heat-related, it's possible that radiation was also involved. Some of the people who approached the wreckage may have later suffered radiation-related illnesses and possibly death.

Examining the crashed object from a safe distance, the remaining cowboys noticed that the ground around the UFO had been strangely affected by the crash. The newspaper said, "When it first touched the earth the ground was sandy and bare of grass. The sand was fused to an unknown depth over a space about 20 feet wide by 30 feet long, and the melted stuff was still bubbling and hissing. Between this and the final resting place there were several other like spots where it had

THE REAL COWBOYS & ALIENS

> **A CELESTIAL VISITOR.**
>
> A Startling and Curious Story from the Ranges of Dundy County.
>
> A Blazing Aerolite Falls to the Astounded Earth.
>
> It is Evidently a Machine of Human Manufacture.
>
> All Particulars that are Yet Learned.
>
> Special to THE STATE JOURNAL.
>
> BENKELMAN, June 7.—A most remarkable phenomenon occurred about 1 o'clock yesterday afternoon at a point thirty-five miles northwest of this place. John W. Ellis, a well known rancheman, was going out to his herd in company with three of his herders and several other cowboys engaged in the annual roundup. While riding along a draw they heard a terrific rushing, roaring noise overhead, and looking up, saw what appeared a blazing meteor of immense size falling at an angle to the earth. A moment later it struck the ground out of sight over the bank. Scrambling up the steep hill they saw the object bounding along half a mile away and disappear in another draw. Galloping towards it with all their speed, they were astounded to see several fragments of cog-wheels and other pieces of machinery lying on the ground, scattered in the path made by the aerial visitor, glowing with heat so intense as to scorch the grass for a long distance around each fragment and make it impossible for one to approach it. Coming to the edge of the deep ravine into which the strange object had fallen, they undertook to see what it was. But the heat was so great that the air about it was fairly ablaze and it emitted a light so dazzling that the eye could not rest upon it more than a moment. An idea of the heat may be gained from the fact that one of the party, a cowboy named Alf Williamson, stood with his head incautiously exposed over the bank, and in less than half a minute he fell senseless. His face was desperately blistered and his hair singed to a crisp.
>
> *The Nebraska State Journal (Lincoln, Nebraska), 6-8-1884, p.5*

come in contact with the ground, but not so well marked."

The only air travel known in 1884 was in hot air balloons, which had no engines and few mechanical parts. It is doubtful that the crash of a balloon could have caused such intense heat or radiation. It is also doubtful that it would have scattered so many strange pieces of metallic machinery all over the crash site.

Another interesting feature of the crashed object was an intense light that continued shining long after the crash. After nightfall, many people from neighboring ranches came to the crash site to view the mysterious object. But, even hours after it fell, the light was still too bright to look at directly. "The light emitted from it was like the blazing rays of the sun and too powerful to be borne by human eyes," the newspaper said.

OLD WEST UFOS: 1865-1895

On the following morning, June 7, 1884, the crash site was again visited by many of the local people. Among the visitors was E. W. Rawlings, an inspector of cattle brands for the local ranches. The wreckage had, by then, cooled a bit, although it was still too hot to touch.

After looking over the crash site, Rawlings went into the nearby town of Benkelman, Nebraska, and he supposedly verified that everything Ellis and the other cowboys had reported was true. The newspaper reported, "Great excitement exists in the vicinity and the roundup is suspended while the cowboys wait for the wonderful find to cool off so they can examine it. Mr. Ellis will go to the land office to secure the land on which the strange thing lies so that his claim to it cannot be disputed."

So, what finally happened to all the debris from this airship crash? In its June 10, 1884 edition, the *Daily State Journal* said, "It is gone, dissolved into the air. A tremendous rainstorm fell yesterday afternoon beginning around 2 o'clock. As it approached, in regular blizzard style, most of those assembled to watch the mysterious visitor fled to shelter, a dozen or more, among them your correspondent, waited to see the effect of rain upon the glowing mass of metal. The storm came down from the north, on its crest a sheet of flying spray and a torrent of rain. It was impossible to see more than a rod through the driving, blinding mass. It lasted for half an hour, and when it slackened so that the aerolite should have been visible it was no longer there. The draw was running three feet deep in water and supposing it had floated off the strange vessel the party crossed over at the risk of their lives.

"They were astounded to see that the queer object had melted, dissolved by the water like a spoonful of salt. Scarcely a vestige of it remained. Small, jelly-like pools stood here and there on the ground, but under the eyes of the observers these grew thinner and thinner till they were but muddy water joining the rills that led to the current a few feet away. The air was filled with a faint, sweetish smell."

The Nebraska State Journal, 6-10-1884, p.4

Skeptics insist that this UFO crash is false because one of the witnesses said that the wreckage included "fragments of cog-wheels," which were common pieces of machinery in the 19th century. However, as we have previously noted, just because he said it looked like cogwheels doesn't mean that they really were cogwheels. He may have just had no other way to describe it.

In the end, we are forced to agree with what one of the newspaper articles from 1884 said, "The whole affair is bewildering to the highest degree and will no doubt forever be a mystery."

Democrat and Chronicle.

Entered at the Post-Office at Rochester, N. Y., as Second-Class Mail Matter.

THAT METEOR.

The meteor of last Thursday evening was a deceptive sort of traveler. A good many who saw it, thought it very near them, and that it dropped down just over on the next farm, or alighted in the adjoining town at farthest. Such observers were in error and they had not learned the way of the visitor. The New York Herald of Tuesday had several communications describing its brilliant appearance, and the writers wonder the New York journals were so slow in notifying their readers of the show. One writer says "It moved slowly across the heavens and was visible for 7 seconds, and I have looked in vain for some account in the daily papers, and am surprised that so rare and beautiful an appearance should have been so little noticed." On the morning after the appearance of the meteor the Democrat and Chronicle published a dispatch stating it was seen in Cazenovia, and on Saturday morning we printed accounts of its appearance from various points. Yesterday letters were received at this office giving an account of the aerial visitor in Orleans county and out on lake Erie.

The meteor was seen all the way from Newton, in New Jersey, to Toronto, Canada. A gentleman who had a view of the passing stranger at Albion says: "I was lying in a hammock on the north side of my house, at the time, reading, and saw the meteor pass from east to west, or very nearly so. I should say it was sixty or sixty-five degrees above the horizon, and apparently moved with about the velocity of a sky rocket. I saw it long enough to call to parties some distance away who also saw it. When I first saw it, it was nearly opposite me to the north. Its appearance was that of a ball of fire some four inches across, with quite a long train."

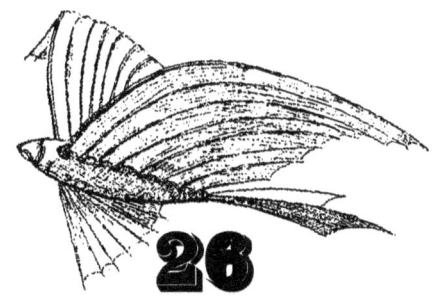

SATURN-SHAPED, MILE LONG UFO
July 3, 1884
Norwood, New York

ON THE EVENING of July 3, 1884, as Norwood, New York, prepared for its annual Independence Day festivities, something incredibly bizarre was seen drifting across the sky over the town. Located in northern New York State, near the Canadian border, Norwood experienced one of the nineteenth century's most interesting sightings of a UFO outside of the 1860 swarm. In his 1923 book *New Lands*, paranormal researcher Charles Fort wrote, "Upon the 3rd of July 1884, a luminous object was seen moving slowly in the sky of Norwood, N.Y. It had features that suggest the structural; a globe the size of the moon, surrounded by a ring; two dark lines crossing the nucleus."

THE REAL COWBOYS & ALIENS

*NASA Photo of a Comet,
Which the 1884 Object Was Not*

As the object swept up from southwest to northwest, residents of other communities in New York State saw it, including at Mount Morris, Wolcott, Clyde, and Waterloo. Although the newspaper accounts refer to the object as a "meteor," eyewitness testimony seems to suggest it was something else altogether. Later, the object was estimated to have been nearly a mile in diameter and flying at an altitude of 115 miles. The incident was impressive enough to draw the attention of Dr. Lewis Swift, one of the leading astronomers of the day.

It was described in the *Democrat and Chronicle* of Rochester, New York, on July 7, 1884: "The reports thus far indicate that the meteor was not seen in the southern or eastern part of the state.

OLD WEST UFOS: 1865-1895

This would show that the meteor was not very high. Most of the observers speak of its apparent nearness to the earth. A gentleman who observed it from Cazenovia Lake writes in the *Syracuse Journal*: "As observed by the writer at Cazenovia lake, this meteor was unusually large, and in the form something like an elongated tear drop, moving perpendicularly. An uncut lead pencil held at arm's length, fairly represents its apparent length. It passed horizontally from east to west and appeared to be nearly as low as the tops of the trees and but a few rods distant; but as it disappeared over the tops of the western hills, its height was of course very great and its distance from the beholder equally so. Yet so bright was the object, so vivid its indescribably brilliant coloring, distinctly marked, that it seemed to be not two rods distant, and to the beholder appeared about to plunge into the side of the hill."

"The light was almost as intense as that of an electric arc light. It moved slowly and was in sight nearly or quite ten seconds. In its wake was left a luminous trail, distinctly visible for several minutes, gradually becoming tortuous and finally breaking up into sections that slowly faded and were lost in the twilight."

"For size and brilliancy, the meteor was not to be compared to that witnessed by the writer in 1860, which passing over Skaneateles lake from the west to east, nearly three hours later in the evening, lighted its shores from hill to hill with almost the brilliancy of daylight. That meteor was observed in many places to the eastward, and also several hundred miles out at sea on the Atlantic, where it made as profound an impression as upon the land. Its beauty, however, was not as striking as the one of Thursday evening. Rarely is such a beautiful object seen in the heavens, and we can only regret that words cannot give an adequate conception of its unearthly beauty."

> **A LARGE METEOR.**
>
> Accounts of the passage of a large meteor from a little north of east to the north west come to us from several localities. Our Clyde correspondent gives a very interesting account of the phenomenon, although he differs somewhat from the observers in this city and Cazenovia, in the direction of the motion. An observer in this city writes to the Democrat and Chronicle as follows: "A large and brilliant meteor passed here in a northerly direction at 8:20 Thursday evening. When first seen by me it was in the east, a little north of east, and about thirty degrees above the horizon. It moved apparently in a right line and disappeared at a point on the horizon northwest by north. The light emitted was white, like that of electric light and so intense as to be plainly seen through the thin and broken clouds. It seemingly had a tail several degrees in length, and owing to the small clouds behind which it passed, it seemed to throw off streamers and fragments like a rocket. It was in sight about two seconds."
>
> Another observer to the north of the city gives substantially the same account. In his judgement the object was very near the earth, as it was shut from view by objects not far distant. Many who saw it thought it was a rocket and did not mention it until they read the report in the telegraphic columns this morning. It was to all appearance moving slowly, but this was only apparent. Its height may possibly be ascertained approximately when reports are received from points to the north and south of us. The light was exceedingly brilliant.
>
> Judging from all the reports, the body itself might have been as large as a hen's egg. Still, it might have been much smaller. When we consider the size and intensity of the light made by one of the little balls from a Roman candle, one may judge how great a light a small piece of meteoric iron set on fire by friction with our atmosphere would produce. The sparks seen in the trail of the meteor were minute fragments of the iron chipped off by the intense heat at the surface. Most of the meteors are so small that they are consumed before reaching the earth. Our atmosphere thus furnishes great protection from the pelting of wandering fragments of matter.

Democrat and Chronicle (Rochester, N.Y.) - July 5, 1884, p. 2

Democrat and Chronicle, July 5, 1884, p.2

In the July 4 issue of the *New York Times*, the object was described as follows: "Cazenovia, N.Y., July 3 -- A magnificent meteor passed from above the pole star to the western horizon at 8:25 o'clock this evening, leaving a trail that remained visible for 10 minutes. Before the trail disappeared, it became sinuous. The light of the trail was much greater than that of the meteor."

OLD WEST UFOS: 1865-1895

> *A METEOR AND ITS TAIL.*
> CAZENOVIA, N. Y., July 3.—A magnificent meteor passed from above the pole star to the western horizon at 8:25 o'clock this evening, leaving a trail that remained visible for 10 minutes. Before the trail disappeared it became sinuous. The light of the trail was much greater than that of the meteor.

N.Y. Times, July 4, 1884, p. 2

In the July 5 edition of the *Democrat and Chronicle*, the following account is found, "A large and brilliant meteor passed here in a northerly direction at 8:20 Thursday evening. When first seen by me it was in the east, a little north of east, and about thirty degrees above the horizon. It moved apparently in a right line and disappeared at a point on the horizon northwest by north. The light emitted was white, like that of electric light and so intense as to be plainly seen through the thin and broken clouds behind which it passed, it seemed to throw off streamers and fragments like a rocket. It was in sight about two seconds."

The Rochester paper continued, "Another observer to the north of the city gives substantially the same account. In his judgement, the object was very near the earth, as it was shut from view by objects not far distant. Many who saw it thought it was a rocket and did not mention it until they read the report in the telegraphic columns this morning. It was to all appearance moving slowly, but this was only apparent. Its height may possibly be ascertained approximately when reports are received from points to the north and south of us. The light was exceedingly brilliant."

In the July 11 issue of the *Democrat and Chronicle*, the strange object was once again discussed: "The meteor of last Thursday evening was a deceptive sort of traveler. A good many who saw it, thought it very near them, and that it dropped down just over on the next farm, or alighted in the adjoining town at farthest. Such observers were in error, and they had not learned the way of the visitor. *The New York Herald* of Tuesday had several communications describing its brilliant appearance, and the writers wonder if the New York journals were slow in notifying their readers of the show.

One writer says, 'It moved slowly across the heavens and was visible for 7 seconds, and I have looked in vain for some account in the daily papers and am surprised that so rare and beautiful an appearance should have been so little noticed.' On the morning after the appearance of the meteor, the *Democrat and Chronicle* published a dispatch stating it was seen in Cazenovia, and on Saturday morning, we printed accounts of its appearance from various points. Yesterday, letters were received at this office giving an account of the aerial visitor in Orleans county and out on Lake Erie."

"The meteor was seen all the way from Newton, in New Jersey, to Toronto, Canada. A gentleman who had a view of the passing stranger in Albion says: 'I was lying in a hammock on the north side of my house, at the time reading, and saw the meteor pass from east to west, or very nearly so. I should say it was sixty or sixty-five degrees above the horizon, and apparently moved with about the velocity of a skyrocket. I saw it long enough to call to parties some distance away who also saw it. When I first saw it, it was nearly opposite me to the north. Its appearance was that of a ball of fire some four inches across, with quite a long train.'"

"The appearance of the meteor at Toronto is described by the *Toronto Mail* as follows: 'At ten minutes past 8 o'clock Thursday night, mean time, a magnificent meteor was observed passing from east toward north at an elevation of about 48 degrees. Its movement was slow, exhibiting brilliant colors of red, yellow and pale green. At about two thirds of its course, an explosion was seen to take place, but no noise was heard. It disappeared behind some church in the north. From the point where the explosion was seen to take place, after all other traces had disappeared, a streak of light vapor extending 20 degrees in length, remained visible for a considerable time until covered by the rapidly increasing cloudiness. The size of the head was five times the diameter of Venus, and the light emanating from the meteor was sufficient to startle many.'"

On July 14 and again on the 18th, the *Democrat and Chronicle* published the results of trigonometric calculations by a gentleman named Irving L. Malany of Clyde, New York, who took the various observations of the eyewitnesses and estimated that the object had a real diameter of "about four-fifths of a mile" [4,224 feet] and that it was travelling 115 miles above the surface of the earth. Outer space officially begins at the Kármán line, an altitude of 100 kilometers (62 miles) above sea level.

Astronomer Dr. Lewis Swift, Expert on Comets

Also on July 14, in the *Buffalo Morning Express*, Dr. Lewis Swift, director of the Warner Observatory in Rochester, appealed to all who saw the July 3rd object to contact him at the observatory to give him "the direction of view, motion, color, etc." Swift, according to the newspaper, wanted to get to the bottom of what exactly the object was. The authors were, unfortunately, not able to find any follow up articles to Dr. Swift's investigations.

```
                    Upon the 3rd of July, 1884, a luminous object was seen
moving slowly in the sky of Norwood, N. Y. It had features that suggest the
structural: a globe the size of the moon, surrounded by a ring; two dark lines
crossing the nucleus (Science Monthly, 2-136).
```

Excerpt from Charles Fort's Book "New Lands" (Archive.org)

OLD WEST UFOS: 1865-1895

In conclusion, the July 3, 1884 object -- because of its size, elevation, motion, shape, color, and other visible characteristics -- was very likely not a meteor at all; however, the observers of 1884 had no other vocabulary they could have used other than "meteor" or "comet." Given that it was nearly a mile in diameter and flying in the lower atmosphere apparently without visibly descending, the object's nature is definitely mysterious. Incredibly bright, the object was described as a "ball of fire," an "elongated teardrop," and a Saturn-shaped globe that looked "structural" in nature. For UFO researchers, this is clearly an unidentified flying object sighting from early in American history.

An Electric Ball.

During last evening's storm a beautiful as well as an awe inspiring scene was presented to the gaze of those so fortunate as to be upon the street at the time. It was just after the flash of lightning and crash of thunder which made every one believe for an instant that he had been struck. No sooner did the thunder peal than a ball of fire, resembling a meteor, shot athwart the zenith, and rolling rapidly to the west, began to descend. Its starting point was in the east, and it began to descend while passing over the city, filling the startled spectator with feelings of terror. It descended rapidly, and as it passed through the air it produced a whizzing, sizzling sound, and threw off numerous sparks in its flight. With terrific force the glaring missile, hurled from some planetary wreck or produced by some strange freak of electricity, struck the Missouri river about a quarter of a mile below the landing, the gurgle and momentary roar of the aggravated waters being plainly heard on west Main street. The strange visitor appeared and disappeared in an instant, and no one will ever know what it was. But as electricity was playing havoc with the elements at the time, it is believed to have been some electric phenomenon.

The Bismarck Tribune, 7-8-1885, p.3

UFO CRASH IN THE MISSOURI RIVER

July 7, 1885
Bismarck, Dakota Territory

ON THE EVENING of July 7, 1885, an intense storm gripped the city of Bismarck, Dakota Territory (now North Dakota), with blinding flashes of lightning, deafening roars of thunder, and torrential rain. Suddenly, there was a particularly bright flash of lightning, followed by an incredibly loud peal of thunder, after which a remarkable sight appeared in the skies over the town. Streaking across the evening sky was a huge fireball, moving east to west and descending rapidly toward the Missouri River below.

An article about what happened appeared in the *Bismarck Daily Tribune* on the following day, in which the object was described as "a ball of fire" that, as it moved over the city, filled "the startled spectator with feelings of terror."

*A Fireball Streaks Across the Sky
(Public Domain)*

Although initially said to resemble a meteor, that opinion quickly changed as the eyewitnesses continued to observe the object's downward trajectory and subsequent splashdown in the waters of the Missouri River.

On its way down to the river, the fireball made an eerie "whizzing, sizzling sound" and threw off numerous sparks, leading observers to suspect that electrical forces were at work within it.

Its landing in the river was quite spectacular, as described in the newspaper: "With terrific force the glaring missile, hurled from some planetary wreck or produced by some strange freak of electricity, struck the Missouri river about a quarter of a mile below the landing, the gurgle and momentary roar of the aggravated waters being plainly heard on west Main street."

OLD WEST UFOS: 1865-1895

The crash landing of this strange mass, which exhibited much sparking and evidence of electrical forces, led the newspaper reporter to conclude that "it is believed to have been some electric phenomenon."

Was it just a case of static electricity built up on the object's surface during its passage through the atmosphere? Or could this strange visitor have been some type of craft that made a "splashdown" in the river in the same manner that U.S. spacecraft splashed down in bodies of water for many years?

Apollo 14 Splashdown (NASA)

The sight of this strange object splashing into the Missouri River was described as "a beautiful as well as awe inspiring scene." It struck the surface of the river with a "terrific force," whose vibrations were heard and felt miles away.

Although one cannot remove from the table the possibility that what crashed here was just a meteor, the eyewitness accounts are unusual enough to suggest that it might have been something else entirely. Perhaps even an interstellar craft from the far reaches of space.

Bismarck, Dakota Territory c.1883
(Library of Congress)

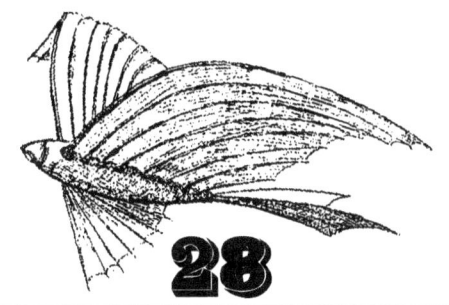

THE SASQUATCH FROM OUTER SPACE

Circa 1888
Humboldt County, California

IN THE WORLD of unexplained phenomena, the big three are undoubtedly UFOs, the Loch Ness Monster, and Bigfoot. Not surprisingly, due to its strange appearance, some people believe that Bigfoot is not native to the Earth and is probably a species that was dropped off upon our planet by visitors from outer space, either as some sort of experiment or because Earth is a convenient dumping ground for unwanted hairy monsters from other planets.

The idea that Bigfoot and UFOs are connected is actually not something new. The first story suggesting Bigfoot was a hairy castoff from a UFO appeared in the late 1800s.

THE REAL COWBOYS & ALIENS

People of the Wild West Period, especially Native Americans, reported seeing large man-like beasts in the wild. Furthermore, almost all Native Americans have legends of hairy giants resembling Bigfoot.

One of the strangest Bigfoot stories of all comes from a journal written by a Mr. Wyatt, a cattleman in California in the 1800s. The incident happened in 1888 in Humboldt County, in the "Big Woods Country," where Wyatt had spent the winter with a Native American tribe. Wyatt had learned to speak the tribe's language and, having gained their trust, was allowed to participate in tribal activities.

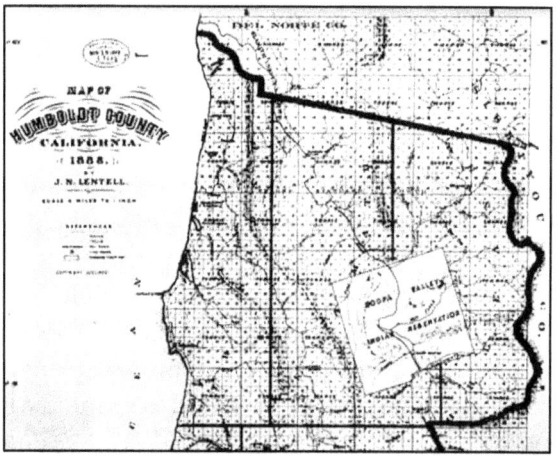

*1888 Map of Humboldt County, California
(National Park Service)*

One day, while out in the woods, Wyatt came across a local tribesman carrying a platter of raw meat. Wondering what was going on, and who the meat was for, Wyatt began to question the man.

OLD WEST UFOS: 1865-1895

Although reluctant at first, the tribesman finally allowed Wyatt to follow him to a nearby shallow cave along a cliff face.

Inside the mysterious cave, a very strange creature sat cross-legged on the ground. The being looked like a man, except that it was very large, muscular and hairy. The man-beast was entirely covered in long, shiny, black hair, except for its palms and an area around its eyes. Also, the creature seemed to have no neck, its head appearing to rest directly upon its shoulders.

A Crazy Bear in its Cave (Art by Jared Olive)

THE REAL COWBOYS & ALIENS

Despite its frightening appearance, the monster did not seem aggressive or dangerous. As Wyatt and the other man approached, the creature sat contentedly, eating its meat. In fact, Wyatt said he went back to visit the creature on more than a dozen occasions. Unfortunately, Wyatt's diary gives no details of his other visits and does not say if he ever tried to communicate with the creature in any way.

Curious about the man-beast, Wyatt asked the tribesmen questions about their mysterious "guest." Finally, after trading one man two pounds of tobacco, an axe, and a compass, one of the tribesmen relented and told Wyatt the origin of their hairy visitor.

The tribesman took Wyatt to a high rock pinnacle and told Wyatt that men came down from the sky in "a small moon" and dropped off several hairy creatures, which the natives called "Crazy Bears," to the Earth. The tribesman said this had happened several times before in the past.

He also said that men from the small moon looked like normal human beings, but they had short hair and wore tight-fitting, silver clothing. According to the tribesman, the men even waved to the tribe in a friendly manner before closing the door to their spaceship and flying away!

After the "Crazy Bears" were dropped off, the tribe would round them up and escort them through their village. The natives at the time believed that the Crazy Bears were capable of "powerful medicine," which is why they fed and cared for them in the nearby caves. The tribesman apparently never told Wyatt what happened to all the other Crazy Bears that had been dropped off in the past, as he only saw one such creature during his time with the tribe.

The Enigmatic Crazy Bear (Art by Neil Riebe)

Why would aliens drop off these Bigfoot creatures on the earth? Wyatt's grandson, James Wyatt, told paranormal investigator Brad Steiger that the aliens may have been conducting some sort of experiment.

Many people believe that Bigfoot may be the descendant of an extinct species of giant ape called *Gigantopithecus*, which stood nine feet tall and was covered in a thick layer of hair. If the Crazy Bears were descended from these ancient apes, perhaps they originated on Earth and not in outer space. Or maybe the visitors who rode the "small moons" picked up the apes, experimented on them, and then returned them to the Earth in a genetically altered condition.

The story of the Crazy Bears is not the only tale to associate Bigfoot with UFOs. Many other Bigfoot sightings have occurred at the same places and times that UFOs were spotted. Some witnesses have even claimed to have seen a Bigfoot creature vanish into thin air, as if it had stepped into another dimension. Perhaps this is why a Bigfoot has never been captured in the wild.

If the story told in Wyatt's diary is true, then perhaps Bigfoot really does come from outer space. In any case, the Crazy Bear story is one of the Old West's most interesting tales concerning UFOs and mysterious creatures.

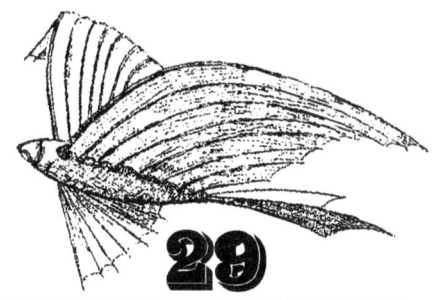

CONNECTICUT UNDERWATER UFO

October 9, 1888
Long Lake, Connecticut

BACK IN 2011, when writing the first *Real Cowboys and Aliens*, the authors were quite intrigued to find a case of an Unidentified Submersible Object (USO). While a UFO is one thing, to find a pioneer era USO case was totally another. And what a doozy of a sighting that one was, occurring in Tacoma, Washington, in 1893, where the USO resembled a strange, mechanical caterpillar. But as our research continued, we found that USO sightings were not quite as uncommon as we thought. Although many researchers think underwater UFOs were responsible for the sightings referenced in this chapter, there remains the possibility that the objects were some kind of biological or semi-biological entities.

In the previous book in this series, *Early American UFOs*, we described an 1813 USO sighting that took place in the Atlantic Ocean. The witnesses said it was a huge "sea monster." However, at 200 feet long, it was much too large to be a living creature, and it also seemed to be inorganic, suggesting that it was some type of vehicle.

Postcard depicting Highland Lake, Circa 1901 (Wikipedia)

The 1888 sighting we are about to discuss, from Long Lake, Connecticut [today Highland Lake], is a more typical USO sighting -- if typical was a word that could be used to describe such sightings. What residents of Long Lake witnessed on that October 9, 1888, evening was described as an intense light moving underneath the water. As already stated, though the 1893 USO sighting was undeniably more entertaining, this sighting as reported in the *Hartford Times*, seems more credible.

OLD WEST UFOS: 1865-1895

The article, entitled "Plowed by Fire" states that, "A most singular scene was witnessed on Long lake during a storm recently.... The lake is three miles long and is divided into three bays. About 3:15 o'clock a vivid flash of lightning illuminated the scenery, followed by a terrific peal of thunder. The wind by this time was blowing with cyclonic force. Suddenly there came a roar, and far down the lake a huge flame of fire could be seen."

Dexter Free Press, 10-26-1888, p.4

What the article describes next sounds like a phenomena that could be generated by a strange craft: "The water for yards ahead was parted as though by a gigantic plow, and the billows seemed to rise at the side of this furrow for fully twenty feet. The ball of fire seemed to force the water aside, and so deep did it go that the bottom of the lake could almost be seen as it passed through the narrows. The parted waters, with their singular propeller, advanced toward the head of the lake with great rapidity. When within one hundred yards of the shore there came another flash of lightning, and the fire disappeared as suddenly as it had come."

The article added, "The residents along the lake who witnessed the strange phenomenon were greatly alarmed. They insist that the ball of fire was fully ten feet long, and half of the mass appeared to be buried in the waters of the lake. It was many hours before the waters of the lake became calm." This USO story sadly seems to have been largely forgotten in modern day Connecticut. Today, about the most interesting local lore regarding the lake is a legend that at some point during the many years that trolley cars serviced the area around the lake, one of the trolley cars fell in and sank to the bottom.

Connecticut Trolley Car (Wikimedia)

According to the article "Could Highland Lake be hiding a trolley?" from *The Registered Citizen*, in 2009 the Highland Lake Watershed Association organized an effort to clean up the bottom of the lake utilizing volunteer scuba divers. It would have made for a very interesting ending to this story if we could have said that while cleaning the bottom of the lake, the scuba divers came upon evidence of the mysterious object that was seen in the lake back in 1888. Unfortunately, that's not what happened. Instead, the divers collected trash from the bottom of the lake and successfully completed their cleanup without encountering any surprises.

One could argue that whatever object was seen moving below the surface of the lake back in 1888 had long since departed the area, returning to whatever nether regions it called home.

THE REAL COWBOYS & ALIENS

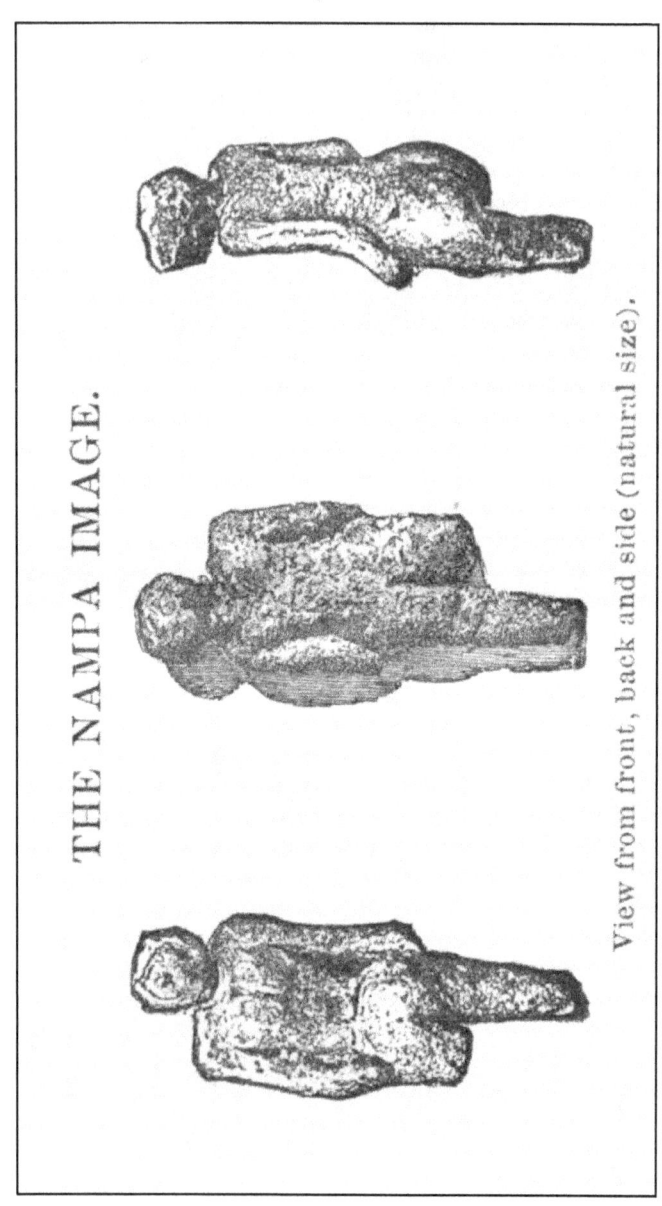

THE NAMPA IMAGE.

View from front, back and side (natural size).

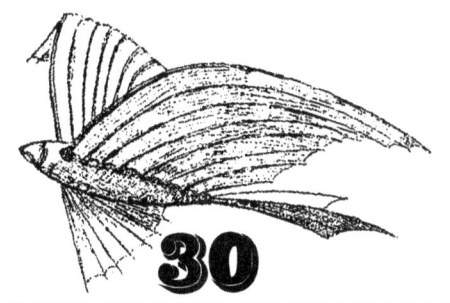

30
ALIEN ARTIFACT UNEARTHED?
August 1, 1889
Nampa, Idaho

FOR MANY PEOPLE, the "holy grail" of UFO research would be the discovery deep underground of an artifact that cannot be explained by human science and that suggests extraterrestrials have visited us in the past. Such a discovery was actually made in August 1889 in the small mining town of Nampa, Idaho, while a deep hole was being dug for an artesian well. The discovery astounded the men of science at that time and continues to be discussed by scientists even today.

As reported in the November 9, 1889 issue of *Scientific American*, around the first of August 1889, Mr. M. A. Kurtz of Nampa, Idaho, was engaged in boring an artesian well in that town, which is located about twenty miles from Boise

City, when he discovered, at a depth of 320 feet, a strange figure, which he described as "apparently the figure of a female, one leg and one arm being [partially] missing, made of baked clay." The object, which is about one and a half inches in length, "came up in the sand pump in the ordinary way from a depth of about 320 feet below the surface."

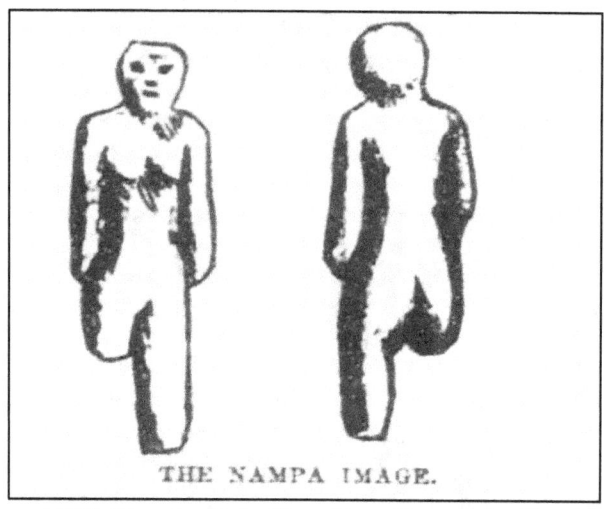

1889 Sketch of Artifact Dug Out of the Earth (Junction City Weekly Union, 12-7-1889, p. 5)

Kurtz was at the dig site watching the progress of the boring, when the contents of the sand pump came out, and he ran his hand through it as it was dumped out. At first, he thought it was just random debris, perhaps "a twig," but after dipping it in a barrel of water to wash the dirt away, he saw the bizarre figure.

OLD WEST UFOS: 1865-1895

Also present at the dig site was Alexander Duffes, described as "a prominent citizen of the town, and the driller and helper." Duffes later gave a report of the different strata he had drilled through before finding the object: "Sixty feet of soil, 12 to 15 feet of lava rock, 100 feet of quicksand, 6 inches of clay, 40 feet of quicksand, 6 feet of clay, 30 feet of quicksand, 12 to 15 feet of clay, then clay balls mixed with sand, then coarse sand in which the image came up, then vegetable soil, then the original sandstone."

Nampa, Idaho - circa 1907

Over the years, skeptics have suggested the figurine was put into the hole by someone during the drilling. But about that possibility, the reporter said, "To the suggestion that the image may have fallen into the well, or been thrown in, it is replied that the hole is tubed with a heavy six-inch pipe from the top, and any light substance thrown in would have been ground to pieces by the action of the sand pump."

Among the first men to handle the artifact, on the day after it was found, was Harvard graduate Mr. G. M. Cumming, general manager of the Union Pacific Railroad in the Nampa district, who expressed his confidence that the discovery was genuine. The figure was then scrutinized by Professor Frederic Ward Putnam (1839-1914), a prominent anthropologist at Harvard University, known today as the "Father of American Archaeology," and Professor Henry Williamson Haynes (1831-1912), a renowned archaeologist from Boston. The two experts stated their opinion that "it was not a clay image, but had been carved from a light pumice stone, and that the coating of red material enveloping it was a cement of oxide of iron that must slowly have collected upon its surface. An evidence of its genuineness exists in some particles of sand cemented into the crease between the arm and the body, which can be seen in the left-hand side of the front view of the accompanying cut. These could not have been where they are if it had been recently manufactured."

Frederic Ward Putnam (Left) and Henry Williamson Haynes (Right)

OLD WEST UFOS: 1865-1895

After completing their investigation, the professors were certain the artifact was the real thing. *Scientific American* proclaimed, "Taking the evidence altogether, Prof. Putnam and Prof. Haynes are entirely convinced of its genuineness."

Regarding the artifact's age, the scientists of the time felt that it was of great antiquity. *Scientific American* said, "The subsequent questions to be determined relate to its age. A communication to Prof. [G. Frederick] Wright from Mr. S. F. [Samuel Franklin] Emmons, of the United States geological survey, expresses it as his opinion that the beds from which the image is supposed to have been derived are probably of far greater antiquity than any deposits in which human implements have heretofore been discovered. The occurrence of the beds is readily accounted for by inspection of the region. Through obstructions in the lower part of the Snake river, probably caused by lava outflows, the water was dammed up and a lake formed. Into this lake the Snake river brought a rapid accumulation of material, doubtless from the melting glaciers near its head waters, so that a comparatively short time, a few hundred years perhaps, or a thousand at most, would be ample for the accumulation of the sediment, when a lava outflow covered over the whole and sealed it up. Doubtless if we could freely excavate the old surface at this great depth many interesting things would be found. The discovery of so good a specimen of art as this Nampa image is adds weight to the evidence which Mr. Whitney has presented, and supports his theory and that of Prof. Putnam that the human race was much farther developed on the Pacific slope in the earliest times than it was on the Atlantic coast or in Europe, and the discovery will bear with strong weight against those who assume an unvarying and gradual evolution of the human species."

The figurine became an important piece of evidence for Creationists, who disbelieve the theory of evolution and who do not think mankind evolved from a lesser species. It also was used to argue in favor of the Biblical account of Noah's Flood, as pointed out by *Scientific American*: "Orthodox theologians would be inclined to regard the image as a relic of antediluvian art [from before the Biblical flood of Noah]."

In his 1956 book *Strangest of All*, paranormal researcher Frank Edwards wrote, "Its very existence resulted in the customary scientific squabbling. To admit that it might be genuine would mean jeopardizing the long-held scientific opinions on the antiquity of man in this hemisphere, so the stand-patters denounced the image as a fraud. But there were so many eminent men of science who came and saw and went away convinced that the Nampa Image was a genuine relic, an artifact tens of thousands of years old, lost ages ago by some Dawn Man in the sandy bed of a stream and brought up in fair condition by an astounding freak of chance. Unfortunately, the argument as to its age cannot be resolved by the carbon-dating technique which is applicable only to organic materials."

OLD WEST UFOS: 1865-1895

Comparison of the Artifact (left) and a Grey Alien (right)

In examining the figure closely, while it looks humanoid, it does not look entirely human. When it was examined by Professor Wright, he commented on the strangeness of the abnormally large head. He said, "The head is large and pushed to one side. It was never carved into any good shape. There are three rude depressions upon the face, suggesting the eye orbits and mouth." That many observers felt the image was that of a female is due to a "slight depression between the breasts." Could this be a depiction of what ancient visitors to the Earth may have looked like? Perhaps it was a crude attempt by an ancient human to create a representation of the extraterrestrials that had suddenly appeared among them with technologies that were beyond belief? Or perhaps this is a figure that the "ancient astronauts" themselves used to represent human beings? The questions are many, but unfortunately, the answers are few.

The fact that this artifact came from 320 feet below the surface and from perhaps hundreds of thousands of years in the past makes its discovery a total mystery. In *The Nampa Image: Correspondence Relating to its Discovery, with Explanatory Comments, etc.* by George Frederick Wright, he reiterates his amazement at the strange figure found in Nampa.

Wright's pamphlet contained the letter he received from Kurtz regarding his discovery of the figure:

> Nampa, Idaho Ter., Oct. 11, 1889.
>
> PROF. G. F. WRIGHT.
>
> DEAR SIR:
>
> Your letter of the fifth at hand and contents noted. In reply would say that the well is tubed with a heavy six-inch pipe from the top and any light substance thrown in would float on the water and be ground to pieces by the sand pump.
>
> We had been getting some of the clay balls and the character of the sand was changing. I had been at the well for several days and ran the contents of the sand pump through my hand as it was pumped out. I had the clay image in my hand and supposed it was a twig. I dipped it into a barrel of water standing near, washed it off and saw at once what it was.
>
> Mr. Duffes, a prominent citizen of our town, happened to be standing by and saw it all. The driller and helper were the only other persons present. If convenient for you, I would be glad to have a brief opinion from you as to your idea of it.
>
> Yours, very truly,
>
> M. A. KURTZ.

Wright's pamphlet also includes a letter from Alexander Duffes, Kurtz's assistant on the drilling project, attesting to the truth of their story, in which he emphasizes that none of the drilling crew could have possibly hoaxed the discovery.

Also included is a letter from railroad executive G.M. Cumming regarding the credibility of Kurtz and Duffes, in which he says, "I have known these gentlemen for some time and in the case of Mr. Kurtz for several years. They are intelligent and well-informed men of the highest character and no one of their acquaintance would hesitate for a moment to accept and believe their testimony on any question of business. In the case of the Nampa image, they would have no motive to mislead the public, even if they were willing to do so.... So far as my own opinion is concerned, I am prepared to accept the image as what it purports to be, namely, as having been found at a depth of more than three hundred feet beneath the lava beds of the Snake River valley."

Nampa, Idaho, Nov. 7, 1889.

M. A. KURTZ, ESQ.

DEAR SIR:

In reply to your inquiry of this date in regard to the facts as regards the finding of the "Baby image" in the Nampa Artesian well, I beg to state the following:

I was present at the well along with yourself and saw you pick it out of the sand as it was discharged from the sand pump.

There were no others present except two men attending the engine and sand pump. And they could not by any means get it into the place where found, and were just as much astonished as ourselves at seeing the find. These are the facts of the case, to which I hereby certify, trusting this will thoroughly quiet all doubts.

I am yours truly,

ALEX. DUFFES.

The historical record also shows that neither Kurtz nor Duffes ever profited in any manner from their discovery, which tends to support the argument that they had absolutely no profit motive in mind for creating a hoax. Given that it seems likely to be genuine and that it has been carefully studied by scientists and scholars for over 150 years, it is remarkable that the origin, age, and purpose of this figurine are still unknown.

Ancient Japanese Figure That May Depict an Extraterrestrial
(By Rc 13 - Own work, CC BY-SA 4.0, https://commons.wikimedia.org/w/index.php?curid=45096686)

Perhaps someday, researchers will discover more of these figures in another highly unusual location. Maybe the context will show that they were, in fact, evidence that the Earth has been visited in the past by extraterrestrials?

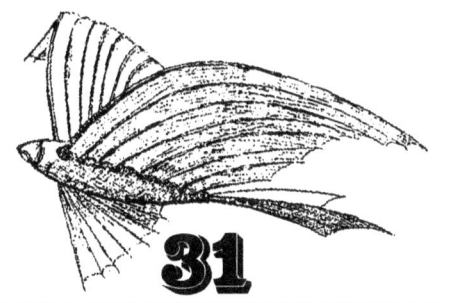

31
THEY CAME FROM THE NORTH POLE
September 16, 1889
Paris, Texas

ON SEPTEMBER 16, 1889, near Paris, Texas, 100 miles northeast of Dallas, one of the most remarkable of the "mystery airship" sightings of the late nineteenth century took place. The incident was first mentioned briefly on September 18, in the *Austin (Texas) American-Statesman*, the *Fort Worth (Texas) Daily Gazette*, and the *Galveston (Texas) Daily News*. The newspaper accounts stated, "Dr. J. M. Stephens, a gentleman of unquestioned veracity, arrived in the city today from Emberson, twelve miles northwest of here, and states that yesterday afternoon, he saw a very large balloon, apparently 100 feet in length, with a car attached, several hundred feet in the air and drifting southward. He watched it for a few moments, when it disappeared in the clouds.

THE REAL COWBOYS & ALIENS

Considerable curiosity has been manifested in the stray airship, as it had not been heard of before nor has it been seen since."

Similar Airship Sighting from 1896

But the brief stories in the Austin, Fort Worth, and Galveston newspapers were only the beginning. A few weeks later (Oct. 14, 1889), the complete details of the case appeared in the *Galveston Daily News*, and the description of what happened was jaw-dropping. In this case, the air vessel appeared to be an actual inflatable balloon, and its occupants seemed to be human; however, there are other aspects of this sighting that are very bizarre, including the theory that the airship came from a previously unknown advanced civilization in the North Pole.

OLD WEST UFOS: 1865-1895

"What the [Adolphus] Greely party [expedition to the Arctic, 1881-1884] and a host of Arctic explorers have vainly sought to learn, whether or not animal and vegetable matter exists at the North Pole, has at last been discovered. Floating vegetation has brought the theory that there was a climate in the Arctic regions where such matter grows. Not only has the theory been proven correct, but we now know human beings in an advance state of civilization inhabit this region."

"It will be remembered that on the 16th of last month, Dr. J.M. Stephens, an eminent physician of Paris, sighted a balloon about ten miles north of here drifting in the clouds. His report created no little excitement at the time, as no one knew of its ascension or has since heard of its sighting. The fact was widely telegraphed by the newspaper reporters of Paris. The news correspondents had not thought of the circumstance for several days until the Frisco [train service from Oklahoma to North Texas] came in today from the Indian Territory."

"John Stokes, a reliable citizen of the Choctaw Nation [Oklahoma] was one of the passengers. He lives between the Kiamshi [Kiamichi] River and Seven Devils Mountains [in Haskell County, Oklahoma]. The reporter has known him for some time, having frequently met him at Decatur [Texas], in this state in the years 1886 and 1887. "Here, you newspaper men are always after news. I can give you some," he said, striking the reporter on the shoulder. He was too excited for introductory remarks. "You see that don't you?"

he continued, as he produced three pieces of gold from his pocket. They were about three inches long and round, being off different sizes. They were very plain, except that the smallest had one, and the other two had three indented circles in them."

> **A Balloon Sighted.**
> Special to the Statesman.
>
> PARIS, September 17.—Dr. J. M. Stephens, a gentleman of unquestioned veracity, arrived in the city to-day from Emberson, twelve miles northwest of here, and states that yesterday afternoon he saw a very large balloon, apparently 100 feet in length, with a car attached, several hundred feet in the air and drifting southward. He watched it for a few moments, when it disappeared in the clouds. Considerable curiosity has been manifested in the stray airship, as it had not been heard of before nor has it been seen since.

Austin American-Statesman, Sep 18, 1889, p. 1

"This money, he said, came from the dumbest looking people you ever saw. On August 16th, last month, they hit close to my house in a balloon, looked like they were about starved. This is some of the money they gave me and my wife for some provisions. They had scandoodles of gold. Hereupon he was plied thick and fast with questions, and the following is the summary of the many things he had to say."

OLD WEST UFOS: 1865-1895

"It was about dinner time, and he was standing in his door at the house when he saw the balloon some distance off. He watched it till it came down about 100 yards from him, and he at once ran to it. Four men stepped out of a very large wooded car or swinging room enclosed on all sides. It was about 10 feet by 12 feet. The queer people saluted him by bowing and, began talking in a language which he could not understand, whereupon they put their hands to their mouths indicating they were hungry and thirsty, and at the same time produced several pieces of this gold, which they held toward him."

> **A LOST AIR SHIP**
>
> Discovered Drifting in the Clouds Near Paris, Tex.
>
> PARIS, Tex., Sept. 17.—As Dr. J. M. Stephens, a prominent physician of Paris, was going to Embayson, about ten miles north of the city, yesterday evening he sighted a large balloon several hundred feet in the air drifting southward. He watched it a short time when it disappeared in the clouds. He says it was a very large balloon, probably 100 feet in length, and that he could plainly see the car. As no one here knows of its ascension or has since heard from it, it has excited much curiosity.

The Galveston Daily News, Sept. 18, 1889, p. 9

"Stokes gave them something to eat and drink, which they consumed with satisfaction. They communicated with hand signs and pointed to the north as the place they came from. They invited him into their airship which contained some queer instruments, maps, stools and places where they had stored provisions."

"The room had three windows and one door. The windows were covered with some transparent material which looked like hide of a very fine texture. The balloon which was two thirds inflated and was supported by three long rods reaching from top to the ground and seemed to be made of the same material."

"The men were dressed in heavy coats and had their hair trained to stand straight and was trimmed in the shape of a cube the shortest part being about an inch long. They were below average size and of very light complexion. Their hair and eyes were black."

"Stokes tried to persuade them to remain longer, but about 3 o'clock in the evening they took something that looked much like rosin, which they burned under a funnel shaped concern. The balloon soon became fully inflated and was ready, but not before he obtained one of the smaller maps, which he had with him."

"Had the reporter not known Stokes to be an honest and sturdy man, he may have doubted the story, but the queer coins and chart are here to show for themselves. The latter leaves no room to believe that the thing was created by Stokes as it is on an unknown material and finely executed, the letters and names on the chart are evidently of Grecian origin. A few of the former are identically the same as Greek letters."

OLD WEST UFOS: 1865-1895

"A comparison of it with a map of the Arctic regions shows that the men are from the North Pole and had some knowledge of the country further south; Kennedy's channel, Peabody Bay and Smith Sound are plainly indicated here. The outlines where the maps break off shows they had a vague idea of Baffin Bay."

"Stokes will make an affidavit to his story, and at the News reporter request will carefully preserve the coins and map as being of rare scientific value. He came down in company with some friends who will attend the federal court and will return home tomorrow. He lives in a wild country, is not very well educated, and did not seem to realize the value of his discovery until he had talked with a News reporter."

This case, which was featured in the June 1964 edition of *True West* magazine, remains unsolved, as no further information about it has been found in the historical record. The authors found references to a person named "J. M. Stephens of Paris, Texas" in several other newspaper articles from 1889, suggesting that he was a real person. No newspaper references to a "John Stokes" of Oklahoma have been found; however, the article does say that Stokes lived "in a wild country."

Could this story have been a hoax? Even those of us with the "will to believe" must concede that it seems likely, especially considering that no lost Greek civilizations have ever been found to be living in the North Pole. Still, it is one of the most fascinating of the airship sightings of the late nineteenth century.

THE REAL COWBOYS & ALIENS

THE GALVESTON DAILY NEWS

A RATHER TOUGH STORY

GIVEN TO A REPORTER BY A "SEVEN DEVILS" MOUNTAINEER.

The Queer People Who Alighted from a Balloon and Exchanged Gold for Grub — From the North Pole.

PARIS, Tex., Oct. 13.—What the Greely party and a host of Arctic explorers have vainly sought to learn, viz: whether or not animal and vegetable matter exists at the north pole, has at last been discovered. Floating vegetation has brought the theory that there was a climate in the Arctic regions where such matter grows. Not only has the theory been proven correct, but we now know human beings in an advanced state of civilization inhabit this region. It will be remembered that on the 10th of last month Dr. J. M. Stephens, an eminent physician of Paris, sighted a balloon about ten miles north of here drifting in the clouds. His report created no little excitement at the time, as no one knew of its ascension or has since heard of its alighting. The fact was widely telegraphed by the newspaper reporters of Paris. THE NEWS' correspondent had not thought of the circumstance for several days until the 'Frisco came in to-day from the Indian Territory. John Stokes, a reliable citizen of the Choctaw nation, was one of the passengers. He lives between the Kiamshi river and Seven Devils mountains. The reporter has known him for some time, having frequently met him at Decatur, in this state, in the years 1886 and 1887.

"Here, you newspaper man are always after news. I can give you some," he said, striking the reporter on the shoulder. He was too excited for introductory remarks. "You see that, don't you?" he continued, as he produced three pieces of gold from his pocket. They were about three inches long and round, being of different sizes. They were very plain, except that the smallest had one and the other two three and ten indented circles in them.

"This money," he said, "came from some of the d—est looking people you ever saw. On the 16th of last month they lit close to my house in a balloon; looked like they were about starved. This is some of the money they gave me and my wife for some provisions. They had 'scadoodles' of gold." Hereupon he was plied thick and fast with questions, and the following is a summary of the many things he had to say:

32
UNIDENTIFIED PREHISTORIC OBJECT

April 20, 1890
Tombstone, Arizona

IT'S A STRETCH to include this story in a book about UFOs, but if it makes the reader feel better, we can say that the winged dinosaur found by two cowboys outside of Tombstone, Arizona, in 1890 is a sort of "Prehistoric Unidentified Flying Object." With a wink and a nod, we plunge into our story.

Tombstone had been made famous back in 1881, during the famous Gunfight at the OK Corral. The local newspaper was appropriately named the *Epitaph*, which also signifies the writing on a tombstone. It was in the April 26, 1890, edition of the Tombstone *Epitaph* that the amazing story of two cowboys that encountered a Pterodactyl was first reported.

THE REAL COWBOYS & ALIENS

A Tombstone Street Scene from 1884

The story goes that on April 20 of the same year, those same two cowboys were riding through the Huachuca desert located between the Whetstone Mountains and the Huachuca Mountains outside of Tombstone. In the long lonely stretch of desert they came upon a weary traveler, or perhaps a weary monster we should say.

On the dusty desert floor was an exhausted creature with a huge pair of wings. The *Epitaph* described it as, "A winged monster, resembling a huge alligator with an extremely elongated tail and an immense pair of wings...The creature was evidently greatly exhausted by a long flight..."

OLD WEST UFOS: 1865-1895

Prehistoric Flying Monster

The story continues that the startled monster took to the sky, and the cowboys pursued it across the desert in an exciting horseback chase. Eventually the creature tired again and fell to the ground. The two cowboys then used their Winchester rifles to shoot at the bizarre dinosaur. The bullets seemed to have little effect, and the monster turned on the men, snapping its long tooth-lined beak at them.

The men backed up their horses and kept their distance from the wounded animal. The *Epitaph* continues, "After a few well directed shots, the monster partly rolled over and remained motionless. The men cautiously approached with their horses snorting in terror and found that the creature was dead."

> **FOUND ON THE DESERT.**
>
> **A Strange Winged Monster Discovered and Killed on the Huachuca Desert.**
>
> A winged monster, resembling a huge alligator with an extremely elongated tail and an immense pair of wings, was found on the desert between the Whetstone and Huachuca mountains last Sunday by two ranchers who were returning home from the Huachucas. The creature was evidently greatly exhausted by a long flight and when discovered was able to fly but a short distance at a time. After the first shock of wild amazement had passed the two men, who were on horseback and armed with Winchester rifles, regained sufficient courage to pursue the monster and after an exciting chase of several miles succeeded in getting near enough to open fire with their rifles and wounding it. The creature then turned on the men, but owing to its exhausted condition they were able to keep out of its way and after a few well directed shots the monster partly rolled over and remained motionless. The men cautiously approached, their horses snorting with terror, and found that the creature was dead. They then proceeded to make an examination and found that it measured about ninety-two feet in length and the greatest diameter was about fifty inches. The monster had only two feet, these being situated a short distance in front of where the wings were joined to the body. The head, as near as they could judge, was about eight feet long, the jaws being thickly set with strong, sharp teeth. Its eyes were as large as a dinner plate and protruded about half way from the head. They had some difficulty in measuring the wings as they were partly folded under the body, but finally got one straightened out sufficiently to get a measurement of seventy-eight feet, making the total length from tip to tip about 160 feet. The wings were composed of a thick and nearly transparent membrane and were devoid of feathers or hair, as was the entire body. The skin of the body was comparatively smooth and easily penetrated by a bullet. The men cut off a small portion of the tip of one wing and took it home with them. Late last night one of them arrived in this city for supplies and to make the necessary preparations to skin the creature, when the hide will be sent east for examination by the eminent scientists of the day. The finder returned early this morning accompanied by several prominent men who will endeavor to bring the strange creature to this city before it is mutilated.
>
> TOMBSTONE EPITAPH: TOMBSTONE, ARIZONA, SATURDAY APRIL 26, 1890

According to the article, the two men measured the creature at 92 feet in length! It also said the monster had only two feet, and the head was eight feet long with strong jaws lined with sharp teeth. Because its wings were folded under its dead body, it was difficult to measure the wings, but the two cowpokes estimated them to be 160 feet from wingtip to wingtip!

They said the creature was completely featherless, and hairless for that matter, and the wings were made of a thick, nearly transparent membrane. The skin was very smooth and could be cut off easily, which is why the men sliced off one of the wing tips to take back to Tombstone with them.

Tombstone, Circa 1881 By C.S. Fly (Wikimedia)

The *Epitaph* concludes, "Late last night one of them arrived in this city for supplies and to make the necessary preparations to skin the creature, when the hide will be sent east for examination by the eminent scientists of the day. The finder returned early this morning accompanied by several prominent men who will endeavor to bring the strange creature to this city before it is mutilated."

But did the men ever succeed in their mission to bring the monster to Tombstone? Maybe and maybe not. There exists a story about a photograph being published in an Old West newspaper [not the *Epitaph*; they checked many times!] of six men standing side by side with outstretched arms. Behind them is a huge bird nailed to a wall, its monstrous wings outstretched and its head hanging limp. The monster, all in all, stretched out to about 36 feet.

There are two problems with this photograph, though. It was supposedly published in 1886, four years before the story of the cowboys killing a winged monster in 1890. Second, no one is able to find this alleged photograph, and researchers have been looking for years. Several claimed to have seen the photograph at one time or another, and Ivan T. Sanderson even claimed to possess a copy of the photo. Only he had loaned it to someone that never returned it.

However, don't get too excited if you search the internet for the photo and think you've found it. Many people aware of the so-called missing pterodactyl photo have attempted to recreate it, and some are quite convincing.

Does the fact that no one, including the modern-day offices of the *Epitaph,* can find the photo mean that either story is a hoax? Not necessarily. While the *Epitaph* may have exaggerated the 1890 monster's wingspan, that doesn't mean there's no truth to the story.

OLD WEST UFOS: 1865-1895

According to the book *Thunderbirds: America's Living Legends of Giant Birds* by Mark A. Hall, the story of the Tombstone winged monster lay pretty much dormant until 1930, when author Horace Bell re-told it in his book *On the Old West Coast*. Years later, in 1969, the story appeared in an issue of *Old West* magazine, which prompted a letter to the editor from Harry F. McClure of Lordsburg, New Mexico, located about 150 miles northeast of Tombstone.

McClure stated in his letter that when he was a youth in Lordsburg, he met the two ranchers that had killed the strange creature in Tombstone in 1890. McClure confirmed that the beast was not a bird, having not a single feather upon it. It looked like a pterodactyl, and, according to McClure's recollection of his conversation with the hunters, the winged monster was never captured or killed – it actually escaped. No photograph of it was ever taken, according to McClure. Interestingly, McClure also claimed the two men told him that the newspapers greatly exaggerated the creature's size, and its wingspan was closer to being only 30 feet!

An active debate ensued on whether McClure's account was factual, since it did not jibe with the original newspaper story. However, this actually gave the story credibility. The fact of the matter is, the monster in the story was far too large to have been any real dinosaur. In real life, the largest pterodactyl wingspan measured around 30 feet.

But from where would such a creature have come? Coincidentally, Lordsburg, New Mexico, is a hotspot for UFO activity. Some residents claim there is a portal in the sky they call the "Lordsburg Door," out of which UFOs appear frequently. Portals like this are sometimes thought to allow travel in space, dimension, and time. Is it possible that a flying dinosaur from Earth's early history flew through the Lordsburg Door and found itself in the 19th century?

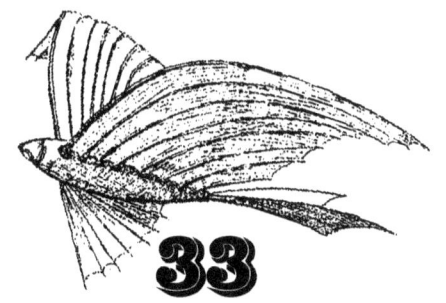

33
CALIFORNIA "METEOR MONSTERS"

April 1891
Yolo County, California

UNDER THE HEADING of UFOs possibly being responsible for dropping off strange beasts like Bigfoot upon the Earth, we have another very early case from Northern California's Yolo County in 1891. A newspaper article caught our eye that mentioned the appearance of "strange monsters" and "falling [celestial] bodies." Appearing in the paper of the town of Woodland, the story in the June 3, 1891 *Woodland Daily Democrat* said, "People around here are afraid to travel the roads above here after midnight for fear of meeting the 'What is it' or getting struck by a meteor. Very likely this valley will be uninhabited in a few years as strange monsters and falling bodies are getting more numerous and bolder each day, and footprints of the monster are now seen as far down the creek as Madison."

> People around here are afraid to travel the roads above here after sunset for fear of meeting the "What Is It" or getting struck by a meteor. Very likely this valley will be uninhabited in a few years, as strange monsters and falling bodies are getting more numerous and bolder each day, and footprints of the monster are now seen as far down the creek as Madison.

Woodland Daily Democrat, 6-3-1891, p.3

Apparently, in the months before, numerous strange "meteors" had zoomed by overhead, after which local people suddenly began encountering a bizarre, furry humanoid wandering around in the woods. The hairy beast sounds an awful lot like our old friends the Crazy Bears, a.k.a. Bigfoot – which makes this yet another early example of people associating Bigfoot-type creatures with UFOs or celestial phenomena.

The sighting of this creature was preceded five months earlier by intense "meteor" activity overhead, including what looked like a "monster meteor" that streaked across the sky before seemingly exploding in a blinding flash of light. According to the *Woodland Daily Democrat* of November 1, 1890: "Persons who were out this morning at 1:20 were surprised to see what appeared to be a very brilliant and blinding flash of lightning in a perfectly clear sky. It was a monster meteor which fell from near the zenith and burst in the southwestern part of the heavens about thirty degrees above the horizon. The appearance of the meteor when it [burst] rivaled that of any human pyrotechnical effect. No audible sound accompanied the explosion." The article added that numerous "meteors" had been seen flying overhead for many evenings. "We are now in the belt of meteors and every evening numbers of them may be seen shooting across the heavens."

Meteor Shower (National Park Service Photo)

Shortly after this intense "meteor" activity, people began to see a very strange creature in the nearby forests, as noted in a *Woodland Daily Democrat* story on April 9, 1891, titled "What Is It?" with the subtitle of "An Unheard-of Monstrosity Seen in the Woods Above Rumsey." As was often the case in stories of this type, the article began by establishing the credibility of the witness, in this case a "Mr. Smith, a well-known citizen of Northern Capay Valley." The reporter states that Smith is an "old acquaintance" of the newspaper and "has always borne a spotless reputation."

"One morning Mr. Smith started out early in quest of game, he had not gone far when his attention was attracted by a peculiar noise that seemed to come from an oak tree that stood nearby. Looking up Mr. Smith was startled to see gazing at him what was apparently a man clothed in a suit of shaggy fur."

Frame from the Patterson/Gimlin Bigfoot Film Footage Taken in Northern California in 1967.

The strange creature had just descended from a tree and exhibited several ape-like behaviors. "Upon reaching the ground, instead of standing upright as a man would, it commenced to trot along on the ground as a dog or any other animal would do."

OLD WEST UFOS: 1865-1895

According to Smith, the creature was "about six feet high when standing, which it did not do perfectly but bent over, after the manner of a bear. Its head was very much like that of a human being. The trapezius muscles [major muscles of the back] were very thick and aided much in giving the animal its brutal look. The brow was low and contracted, while the eyes were deep set, giving it a wicked look. It was covered with long, shaggy hair, except the head, where the hair was black and curly."

Smith hesitated to shoot the strange creature on the spot, thinking it might be a "wild man," who had lived so long in the wilderness that it hardly seemed human anymore. But, attempts to communicate with the man-thing were unsuccessful and only seemed to anger the creature, which bellowed out "grunts of unmistakable anger." Concerned for his safety, Smith fled the scene and headed back to his camp. Smith told his hunting companions of his encounter. "They were disposed to laugh at him at first, but his [sincerity] of manner and the blanched cheeks soon proved to them that he had seen something out of the usual order of things."

Returning to the scene of Smith's encounter, with guns and hunting dogs, Smith and his companions saw a gruesome sight – the beast was eating some small animals that Smith had previously killed and left in a bag. "The creature would plunge its long arms or legs into the bag and pulling forth the small game that was in it, transferred it to its mouth in a most disgusting manner."

THE REAL COWBOYS & ALIENS

The dogs were too frightened of the beast to attack it, and instead began whining loudly, which caused the furry monster to begin making "the most unearthly yells and screams" and then flee into the undergrowth with the hunters in close pursuit.

As if to discourage the hunters from giving chase, the creature "beat its breast with its hairy fists" and broke off a large tree branch, holding it over its head in a threatening manner. The display of aggression had its intended effect, as the hunters decided to give up the chase and return to camp.

According to the newspaper, the wild beast encountered by the hunters could have been the cause of many sheep and hogs disappearing in the area. The article noted that their disappearance might be "traced to the hiding place of the 'What Is It.'"

A few weeks later, on May 21, the *Woodland Democrat* reported the finding of "enormous" footprints near the same area. The newspaper reported, "A party of young men who were fishing on Cache Creek Sunday were thrown into a state of great excitement by the discovery of a lot of mysterious footprints in the sand on the bank of the creek. The tracks were enormous size, of peculiar and outlandish formation and at once excited the apprehension that the mysterious "What is it" of Capay Valley had found his way to that locality."

"The party, thoroughly alarmed, at once secured a number of Winchesters and instituted a search for the animal. Several hours were diligently spent in a fruitless endeavor to capture the wonderful beast ..."

The article closes with a joke about the enormous footprints belonging to a group of local "belles" that had been bathing in the area. As could be expected, several days later, some women who lived in the area wrote a letter to the editor demanding to know the name of the "brute" who suggested that their feet were so deformed. Regardless of this tomfoolery, the newspaper account is still very interesting and seems to generally confirm the previous sighting by Smith and his colleagues.

Since the sightings of this strange creature seemed to diminish afterward, is it possible that whatever entities dropped the creature on Earth later came back for him? About a year later, again strange "meteors" began appearing in the area. On March 18, 1892, according to an article in the *Woodland Daily Democrat*: "A little after ten o'clock Wednesday night, says the *Record Union*, the city and surrounding country was lighted up by an immense meteor that shot apparently almost straight down from the heavens in a northwesterly direction from the city."

"It left a long trail of sparks in its wake, like a comet, the body having a reddish-fiery appearance. Some of those who witnessed the phenomenon declared that the thing came so close that they could hear the hissing sound it made in its descent."

"One man was positive that it struck the earth in the vicinity of Bryte's dairy, a couple of miles up the river, and all declare it to have been the most brilliant meteor they had ever seen."

Interestingly, after that, there were no more reported sightings of the strange, furry monster.

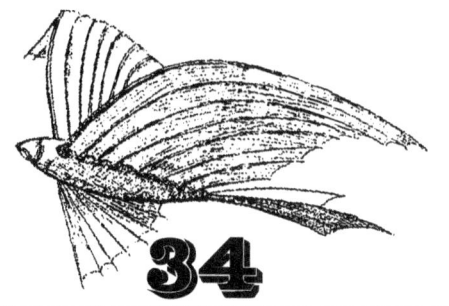

34
UFO EXPLOSION IN TEXAS
June 13, 1891
Dublin, Texas

IN JANUARY 2008, several residents of Erath County in North Texas saw a huge UFO in the skies above them. The object, estimated to be about half a mile long, was seen near the towns of Stephenville and Dublin, Texas. After this happened, some of the older residents remembered a UFO case that took place many years earlier, back in 1891. That was when a flying object exploded in the sky above a local cotton gin.

The UFO sighting took place on Saturday, June 13, 1891, a quiet summer day, in the small town of Dublin. At that time, the town had a population of about 2,000 people, and one of its major businesses was the Wasson & Miller flour mill and cotton gin.

THE REAL COWBOYS & ALIENS

The gin was closed for the weekend, and several townspeople were out for a walk near it when they suddenly noticed something very unusual in the sky above the gin. Witnesses saw a bright, oblong-shaped object hovering about 300 feet up.

Illustration of Explosion over Cotton Gin

An eyewitness, whose name was not given, told the local newspaper that what he saw looked like "a bale of cotton suspended in the air after having been saturated in kerosene oil and ignited, except that it created a much brighter light."

The witness said that the light was so bright that it "dazzled" people who were standing several hundred feet away from the light. This is a mystery, since in the year 1891, bright artificial lights did not exist. Although electric light bulbs had been invented a few years before, they were not widely available yet.

OLD WEST UFOS: 1865-1895

In the 1890s, the most common sources of light were kerosene lamps and campfires. Neither of these was very bright.

> **A Meteor Explodes in the City—An Eye Witness Describes the Scene to a Progress Reporter—Scared.**
>
> Quite a little excitement was created last Saturday night by the bursting of what is supposed by those who were present to have been a meteor, near Wasson & Miller's gin. Quite a number witnessed the explosion and nearly everyone in that portion of the city heard the report eminating therefrom, which is said to have sounded somewhat like the report of a bomb-shell. Our informant (who, though a little nervous at times, is a gentleman who usually tells the truth, but did not give us his statement with a view to its publication) says he observed the meteor when it was more than three hundred feet in the air, before bursting, and that it bore a striking resemblance to a bale of cotton suspended in the air after having been saturated in kerosene oil and ignited, except that it created a much brighter light, almost dazzling those who percieved it. The gentleman in question seems to have been so badly frightened that it was utterly impossible to obtain an accurate account of the dimensions and general appearance of this rare phenomenon, but we are convinced from his statements that his position at the time must have been very embarrassing and that very little time was spent in scientific investigations. However, on the following morning he returned to the scence so hastily left the previous night, to find the weeds, grass, bushes and vegetation of every description for many yards around the scene of the explosion burned to a crisp, also discovering a number of peculiar stones and pieces of metal, all of a leaden color, presenting much the appearance of the lava thrown out by volcanic eruptions. He also picked up some small fragments of manuscript and a scrap, supposed to be part of a newspaper, but the language in both was entirely foreign to him, and, in fact, no one has yet been found who has ever seen such a language before, hence no information could be gained from their examination. At this juncture your reporter requested that he be shown these wonderful fragments of such a miraculous whole, but the narrator had worked himself up to such a pitch of excitement that it was impossible to get him to grasp the significance of our request, and were compelled to leave him a victim to his own bewildered fancy and to ruminate the seemingly miraculous story he had just related. Thus was a repotorial zealot denied the boon of seeing fragments of the most remarkable substance ever known to explode near Wasson & Miller's gin.
>
> P. S. Since the above was put in type we learn that our reporter was given the above information by a contributor to the Dublin Telephone, but the information came too late to prevent its insertion in this paper.

Original Newspaper Article from 1891
(Courtesy of Mark Murphy)

Some people think that the brilliant light might have been caused by an electrical fire or explosion inside the UFO. Maybe the flying object had overheated, causing it to glow brightly before the whole thing blew up in the sky.

Although the local newspaper later described it as a "meteor," the UFO did not look or behave like a meteor. It seemed to "hover" over the gin, and it gave out an extremely intense light. Also, it shattered into pieces *before* it hit the ground.

The witness continued watching the bright light until the flying object suddenly exploded. After the explosion, chunks of a strange, burning-hot metal fell to the ground, setting the grass and weeds on fire. The explosion of the UFO was so loud that it was heard by "nearly everyone in that portion of the city," according to the newspaper.

The man who witnessed this event was so scared by what he saw that he ran away from the gin and hid himself. Later, when he was asked to provide the exact size and appearance of the UFO before it exploded, he could not. He said he was too scared to pay close attention.

After returning to his home, the witness continued thinking about the UFO and was not able to sleep well. He decided that he would return to the scene of the explosion early the next morning – Sunday, June 14, 1891.

The witness was embarrassed at having run away, and he wanted to conduct an investigation into what happened. When he went back, his eyes beheld an amazing sight. Scattered across a field of burned grass and weeds were strange pieces of metal. He described them as "fragments of the most remarkable substance ever known to explode." The metal was of the same color as lead. He also saw some "peculiar stones" that looked like lava from a volcano. And there was something else – even more mysterious. As the witness looked around, he found several small pieces of what looked like paper with strange writing on it.

OLD WEST UFOS: 1865-1895

It looked like torn pieces from a newspaper, but the writing on it was not English. In fact, nobody could identify what language it was. "The language ... was entirely foreign to him, and, in fact, no one has yet been found who has ever seen such a language before," said the report about the incident, which appeared later in the *Dublin Progress*.

Illustration by Neil Riebe

After finding the scraps of paper with the strange writing, the witness became completely "bewildered." The newspaper reporter said that the witness "worked himself up to such a pitch of excitement" that he could not answer any more questions. He would not show any of the wreckage to the reporter or talk any more about it.

The cotton gin where the UFO exploded still exists today. The local museum in Dublin, Texas, hopes to restore the building and preserve it as a historical landmark. Dublin is well known in Texas as the town where the soft drink known as Dr.

THE REAL COWBOYS & ALIENS

Pepper got its start. The very first Dr. Pepper bottling plant was built there in 1891.

Until now, nobody has tried to find any of the strange pieces of metal that fell to the ground. Some of the fragments may still be there, buried under the surface. It is possible that someday, the material will be found. In addition, nobody has ever found traces of the paper with the strange writing on it. Maybe it still exists today in somebody's attic?

Recent Photo of the Old Cotton Gin (Right), Courtesy of Mark Murphy

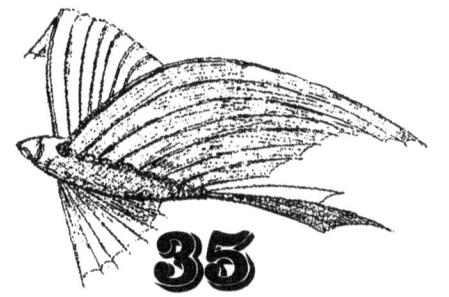

35
THE CRAWFORDSVILLE MONSTER

September 5, 1891
Crawfordsville, Indiana

BACK IN THE 1800s there weren't really any serious UFO researchers like we have today. One of the first persons to begin seriously gathering together stories about strange creatures and unidentified flying objects was Charles Fort.

Born in 1874, Fort began at an early age collecting old newspaper articles, specifically anything that seemed out of the ordinary. Fort eventually published his collected stories and comments in several books. As a result, people began to refer to unexplained happenings as "Fortean events." In similar manner, strange creatures are often called Fortean monsters.

THE REAL COWBOYS & ALIENS

One such Fortean monster believed to possibly be from outer space was the flying monster of Crawfordsville, Indiana, seen on September 5, 1891. Fort read about the beast in the September 10th edition of the *Brooklyn Eagle*. He was so perplexed by the creature's odd, ungainly appearance that he assumed it to be a hoax. To see if this was the case or not, Fort wrote a letter to one of the eyewitnesses mentioned in the newspaper. To Fort's surprise, the man, Reverend George W. Switzer, replied to him and told him that it really happened!

Reverend Switzer (1854-1940) was actually quite active in the affairs of his church, as evidenced by a number of Methodist Church publications we examined for the time period in which he served the church. The historical record shows that he entered the ministry in 1880 and served as minister in Crawfordsville from 1891 to 1893. He then became the superintendent of the Lafayette, Indiana, district.

The story of the strange "sky monster" seen by Switzer was originally reported in the *Crawfordsville Daily Journal* in September of 1891, and it went as follows.

It was midnight on Saturday, September 5, 1891, and Switzer, then 37, had gotten up to get some water from his well when he saw what was surely the strangest sight of his life.

Snaking through the air was an almost formless creature comprised of hundreds of white fluttering fins. Reverend Switzer awakened his wife, Lida, 33, who also got to see the creature. They both said it was, "[swimming] through the air in a writhing, twisting manner similar to the glide of some serpents."

At one point the couple described the monster as swooping so close to the ground that it nearly touched the yard of a nearby home before it continued its flight over the town.

The Crawfordsville Monster (Neil Riebe)

Reverend Switzer's account appeared in the *Crawfordsville Daily Journal* on Monday, September 7, 1891 on page 5: "Shortly after midnight, [Switzer] stepped into his back-door yard to get a drink at the well. As he stood there a strange weird sensation crept over him and although he is unable to say whether he was attracted by any sound or not he suddenly felt his attention drawn upward, and raising his eyes with the full expectation of beholding something, he saw what both puzzled and astonished him. The night was very dark and very still, no breath of air stirring, but propelled by some unseen force he saw sweeping toward him from the southwest the apparition. It was about 16 feet long and eight feet wide, resembling a mass of floating drapery.

'Shaped like a fleecy, milk white cloud, or like a demon in a shroud.'"

Switzer's account continued, "It was much too low to be a cloud and moved far too swiftly, besides there was no wind at all. It seemed to work about as it swam through the air in a writhing, twisting manner similar to the glide of some serpents. Mr. Switzer called his wife out and they watched it until [it] got just east of the church when it began to descend as though about to land in the yard of Mrs. J. M. Lane. They then lost sight of it for the moment, but Mr. Switzer proceeding into the street saw it arise again and he and his wife watched it circle about town for some time, finally tiring and going into the house with the strange phenomenon still visible."

The good reverend and his wife weren't the only ones to see the monster that night. So did two ice delivery men, Marshall McIntyre and Bill Gray, who had gotten up early to prepare their wagon for delivery rounds for later in the morning. Their sighting was actually the first one to be published in the local paper, having appeared on Saturday, September 5. It was about 2 a.m. on Saturday as the two were preparing the ice delivery wagon, when all of a sudden, a feeling of "awe and dread" overcame them.

Turning their heads to the sky, they saw a monster that they described as, "about eighteen feet long and eight feet wide and moved rapidly through the air by means of several pairs of side fins. . ... It was pure white and had no definite shape or form, resembling somewhat a great white shroud fitted with propelling fins. There was no tail or head visible but there was one great flaming eye, and a sort of a wheezing plaintive sound was emitted from a mouth which was invisible. It flapped like a flag in the winds as it came on and frequently gave a great squirm as though suffering unutterable agony."

The two men, who said the monster hovered about three to four hundred feet in the air above them, were able to observe the creature for a whole hour. Eventually the two got scared, harnessed their horses, and left the area.

Several paranormal researchers, including Jerome Clark, have written that on the night after the initial sighting, about 100 local townspeople in Crawfordsville went out late at night hoping to see the creature again and actually did. The monster flew over them and at one point descended so low that they could feel its hot breath.

The September 12th edition of the *Crawfordsville Weekly Journal* noted that letters were pouring in from all over asking or commenting about the strange monster sighting. "Postmaster Bonnell is receiving letters every mail from people all over the country anxiously inquiring about the 'spook' which was seen here last Friday night. The inquiries seem for the most part to be deluded fools and nearly scared out of their wits by what they think portends the approach of Judgment Day."

The paper also stated, "Rev. G. W. Switzer is receiving inquiries from all over the country relative to the 'spook' which he saw Friday night.

THE REAL COWBOYS & ALIENS

The anxious inquiries want to know all about it and Mr. Switzer's personal experience. He received one letter from Keeley's Institute for Inebriates at Plainfield ... advising Mr. Switzer to come on at once for treatment." There was one skeptical note sounded a few days after the sighting of the creature. Two Crawfordsville men came forward and told the local newspaper that they followed the monster as it drifted out of town. Eventually, they were able to ascertain that the so-called "monster" was merely a huge flock of birds known as "killdeers." The two men, John Hornbeck and Abe Hernley, said the birds' many wings accounted for the "fins" of the monster, and their collective shrieking accounted for the mysterious noise. The *Crawfordsville Journal* further speculated that low visibility in the damp night air caused the misidentification and that newly installed electric lights in the town caused the birds to become frenzied.

While it's tempting to shout, "Case closed!" one must remember that while the bird explanation sounds somewhat plausible, it does not explain one important feature of the Crawfordsville monster -- the large, single, flaming eye! All the witnesses claimed to have seen that horrific eye.

And as for some further validation of our key witness's character and intelligence, an interesting account of Reverend Switzer's life appears on the web site *HistoricalCrime-Detective.com*, in explaining that Switzer helped solve the murder of a Crawfordsville preacher's wife, Hattie Pettit.

OLD WEST UFOS: 1865-1895

Reverend George W. Switzer in His Later Years, Courtesy Tippecanoe County Historical Association

The article says, "The Rev George Switzer is critical to the case because of his efforts to bridge the gap between popular and official justice. He was the most influential member of the North-West Indiana Conference of the Methodist church for several decades, and served as a preacher in Shawnee Mound, Crawfordsville, West Lafayette, and many other stations. He first met [William] Pettit [the murdered woman's husband] in 1886 when the latter was ordained, and then handed over the Shawnee Mound congregation to Pettit in late 1887. He then served as Crawfordsville Methodist preacher until 1893. Additionally, he was a member of the Lafayette and Crawfordsville Lodges, and was active as well in the Knights Templar." The article goes on to say that Switzer suspected Mrs. Pettit had been murdered by her husband, a fellow Methodist minister and also a fellow Mason. Switzer badgered authorities until they finally tried and convicted the husband.

The article closes in this manner, "Switzer went on to have an illustrious career in the Lafayette area. He served as Presiding Elder for the Conference until 1909, when he became a banking executive and a DePauw University trustee. Today he is best known as one of several witnesses to a UFO-type sighting that occurred in Crawfordsville in September 1891."

So just what was this flying monster? Many paranormal researchers today think it was an "atmospheric beast" -- a sort of gaseous living organism. Famous scientist Carl Sagan even speculated such creatures could exist on gas planets like Jupiter.

A Fortean investigator living in Crawfordsville, Vincent P. Gaddis, has done more research on the monster than anyone and has concluded, "All the reports refer to this object as a living thing -- in other words, one of the hypothetical atmospheric life forms that would figure in early theories about unidentified flying objects."

A STRANGE PHENOMENON.

A Horrible Apparition Hovers Over the City at an Early Hour this Morning.

What Tam O'Shanter saw on his famous ride was discounted this morning about two o'clock by what Marshall McIntyre and Bill Gray saw. They were at that hour at the barn of William Martin, on east Main street, hitching up the team to the ice wagon preparatory to leaving for the ice houses. While standing in the alley back of the stable Mr. McIntyre suddenly felt a strange sensation of awe and dread coming over him and looking up he saw a horrible apparition approaching from the west. It was about three or four hundred feet in the air, and most greusome in aspect. It was about eighteen feet long and eight feet wide and moved rapidly through the air by means of several pairs of side fins which it worked most sturdily. It was pure white and had no definite shape or form, resembling somewhat a great white shroud fitted out with propelling fins. There was no tail or head visible but there was one great flaming eye, and a sort of a wheezing, plaintive sound

Crawfordsville Daily Journal, 9-5-1891, p.8

An Uncanny Monster.

The people residing along Palmetto creek, South Carolina, as well as those for miles back in the "slashes," are highly excited over the appearance of a strange and uncouth creature in that vicinity. The beast is described as being a creature that far outdoes the nightmare ideas of the mythologists. It is equally at home in the water, on the land or among the tall trees of the neighborhood, where it has been most frequently seen. The general contour of the head reminds one of some gigantic serpent with this exception: The "snout" terminates in a bulbus, monkey faced knot, which much resembles the physiognomy of some gigantic ape. From the neck down, with the exception of some fin shaped flippers, which extend from the arms to the waist, the creature resembles a man, only that the toes and fingers are armed with claws from two to six inches long.

Tracks made by the beast in the soft mud around Hennis lake have been taken to Donner's Grove, where they are kept on exhibition in a druggist's showcase. Those who have seen the horrid thing face to face say that it is a full nine feet in height, which could hardly be believed only for the fact that the tracks mentioned above are within a small fraction of fifteen inches in length. Fishermen who surprised the monster sitting silently on a mass of driftwood declared that its back looked like an alligator's, and that it had a caudal termination a yard long, which forked like the tail of a fish.—St. Louis Republic.

Lawrence (Kansas) Daily Journal, 7-6-1892, p.2

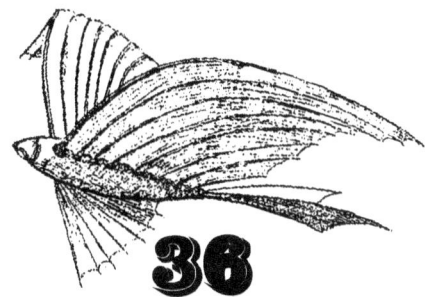

36
THE FIRST REPTILIAN
July 1892
Palmetto Creek, South Carolina

IN JULY 1892, a very unusual creature, belonging to no known Earthly species, was spotted in the wilderness around Palmetto, South Carolina. Described by witnesses as a "strange and uncouth creature," the beast was generally humanoid in appearance, perhaps 9 feet tall, and having a head with the contours of a serpent's head and an ape-like snout. Extending from the arms to the waist, the humanoid had "fin-shaped flippers," and finally, its toes and fingers were armed with "claws from two to six inches long."

To students of Ufology, the description is identical to that of a rumored species of extraterrestrial known as the Reptilian, which makes this 1892 case probably the earliest recorded sighting of a Reptilian.

Alternately known as reptoids, lizard people and Draconians, these extraterrestrials are said to resemble human beings, but are covered in scales and have claws, sharp teeth, and in some cases, tails. These beings are alleged to have the ability to shapeshift into human form to walk among us and to influence human affairs. Supposedly they originate from the Alpha Draconis star system, and secretly control much of the power and influence in human society, hiding out in an underground base while their agents take the guise of important human leaders, including heads of state, military officials, chief executive officers of global corporations, and more. Among the heads of state that have been accused of being Reptilians are Donald Trump, George W. Bush, and Elizabeth II, Queen of England!

In terms of Ufology, the Reptilians are one of the newer alien races to come to light and were popularized by researcher David Icke, the main proponent behind the theory that several key world leaders are disguised Reptilians. The first case of a Reptilian encounter is said to have occurred in Ashland, Nebraska in 1967. A police officer, Herbert Schirmer, claimed that he was abducted by humanoids with a reptilian appearance. The beings even wore a winged serpent emblem on their chests. Though many people today disbelieve Schirmer's story, the incident encouraged other witnesses to come forward with their own stories of having encountered Reptilian-like beings.

OLD WEST UFOS: 1865-1895

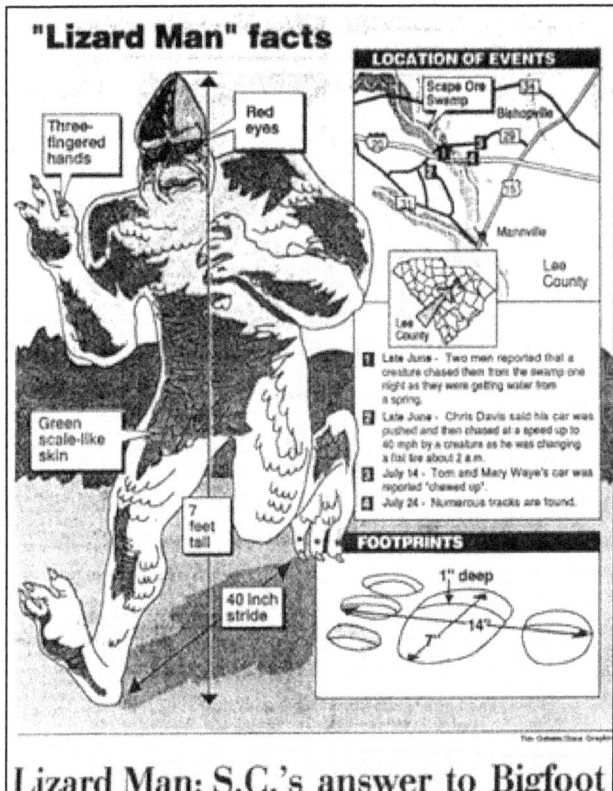

Depiction of Lizard Man from Columbia (SC) State, August 15, 1988

But returning to 1892, the following article was published in many newspapers throughout the United States during the summer of 1892. One of the earliest publications of the article was in the *Lawrence (Kansas) Daily Journal* on July 6, 1892. The story, titled "An Uncanny Monster," states, "The people residing along Palmetto creek ... as well as those for miles back in the slashes,' are highly excited over the appearance of a strange and uncouth creature in that vicinity."

Strange was an apt description, as it was unlike any monster sighted before. The paper declared that the monster "far outdoes the nightmare ideas of the mythologists. It is equally at home in the water, on the land or among the tall trees of the neighborhood, where it has been most frequently seen. The general contour of the head reminds one of a gigantic serpent with this exception: The 'snout' terminates in a [bulbous], monkey faced knot, which much resembles the physiognomy of some gigantic ape. From the neck down, with the exception of some fin shaped flippers, which extend from the arms to the waist, the creature resembles a man, only that the toes and fingers are armed with claws from two to six inches long."

Encouragingly, physical proof was found in the form of the creature's footprints. "Tracks made by the beast in the soft mud around Hennis lake have been taken to Donners Grove, where they are kept on exhibition in a druggist's showcase. Those who have seen the horn'd thing face to face say that it is a full nine feet in height, which could hardly be believed only for the fact that the tracks mentioned above are within a small fraction of fifteen inches in length. Fishermen who surprised the monster sitting silently on a mass of driftwood declared that its back looked like an alligator's, and that it had a caudal termination a yard long, which forked like the tail of a fish."

Although some might argue this story could have been a hoax by the newspaper to increase circulation, it seems odd that the description of the creature almost exactly matches the description of Reptilians given by eyewitnesses who first began encountering them nearly 100 years later!

How could newspapermen, attempting to perpetrate a hoax, have arrived at the very description of a Reptilian that would be given many years in the future? Why not just make up a creature with a man's body but an alligator's head?

There is another factor in this article's favor. About 100 years later the thing, or a member of the same species, was seen again in Scape Ore Swamp, also located in the state of South Carolina. In 1988 a young man named Christopher Davis was driving along a lonely road when he got a flat tire. Just like a scene in a horror movie, as soon as he was done fixing his tire, a nightmarish creature walked onto the road before him.

It was basically the same creature in description as the one from 1892. Davis jumped back into his car and the Lizard Man soon jumped on it! Davis drove off with the thing on the roof and slammed on his brakes in an effort to throw it off. It worked, and the Lizard Man tumbled to the pavement, allowing Davis to make his escape. When Davis told his story to the press, it briefly became a nationwide sensation.

So, was the strange creature seen in 1892 and again in 1988 some kind of reptilian-like humanoid from outer space? Or perhaps they could be some type of previously unknown species that possibly evolved from Earth's early reptiles? In 1982, the curator of vertebrate fossils at the National

THE REAL COWBOYS & ALIENS

Museum of Canada in Ottawa, Dale A. Russell, put forth the interesting hypothesis that if certain types of dinosaurs hadn't gone extinct, they may have evolved into a more humanoid form. Russell called this evolved humanoid reptile a "dinosauroid." And guess what, in Russell's opinion, they would look exactly like a Reptilian E.T.

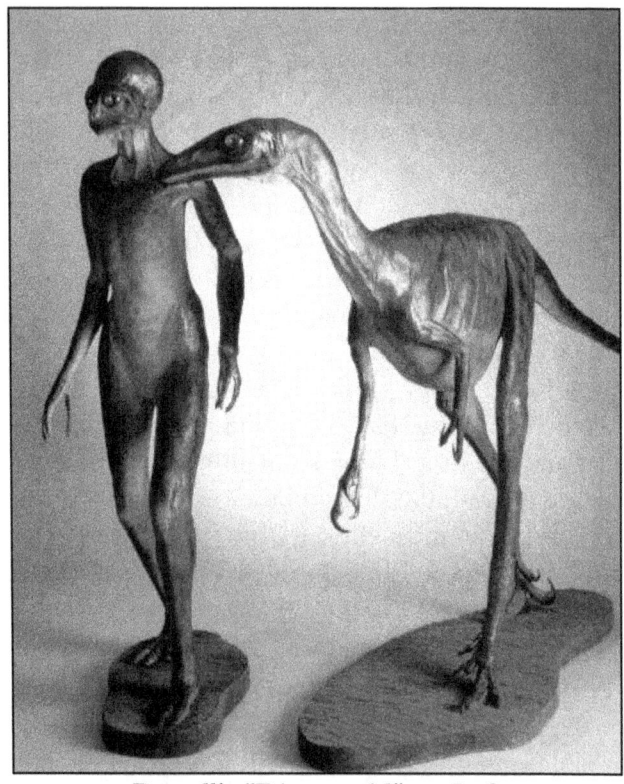

Russell's "Dinosaurid" on Left.

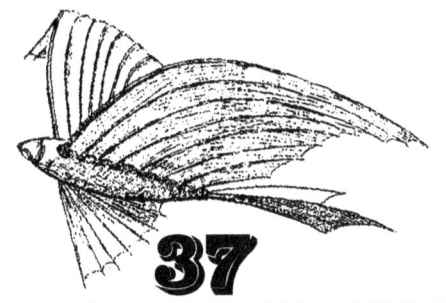

ALIEN SUBMARINE OR MONSTER OF THE DEEP?

July 2, 1893
Tacoma, Washington

WHAT FOLLOWS will surely be considered one of the odder chapters in this book as it covers a very early sighting of an unidentified submersible object (USO), and an especially odd one at that.

It occurred near Tacoma, Washington, on July 2, 1893. The story began on a Saturday afternoon (July 1) at about 4:30 when a group of "well-known gentlemen" departed Tacoma on a boat called *Marion* for a three-day fishing and hunting excursion. A newspaper article said, "The party consisted of Auctioneer William Fitzhenry, H.L. Seal, W.L. McDonald, J.K. Bell, Henry Blackwood and two eastern gentlemen who are visiting the coast."

THE REAL COWBOYS & ALIENS

After several hours of fishing on the Puget Sound, the men decided to go ashore at a place called Black Fish Bay on Henderson Island, where they would camp and spend the night. As it turned out, they made camp within 100 yards of a group of men who were engaged in surveying the area.

Around midnight, one of the fishermen awoke suddenly. He later told a local newspaper, "It was, I guess, about midnight before I fell asleep, but exactly how long I slept I cannot say, for when I woke it was with such startling suddenness that it never entered my mind to look at my watch, and when after a while I did look at my watch, as well as every watch belonging to the party, it was stopped."

He had been awakened by a very loud noise. "I was in the midst of a pleasant dream, when in an instant a most horrible noise rang out in the clear morning air, and instantly the whole air was filled with a strong current of electricity that caused every nerve in the body to sting with pain, and a light as bright as that created by the concentration of many arc lights kept constantly flashing."

Because of the loud noise and electric charge in the air, the witness thought that the fishermen were caught in the middle of an intense thunderstorm. But, looking up at the sky, he saw no evidence of lightning and instead, he noticed strange lights coming from the water of the nearby bay.

By now, the other fishermen and the surveyors were awake and could also see the disturbance occurring in the water. Approaching the shore towards the frightened group was what the witness later described as "a most horrible-looking monster."

Artist's Conception by Neil Riebe

The "monster fish," as they called it, was 150 feet long, but the description sounds more like a giant caterpillar than a fish. The beast had a head that resembled a walrus, but with six eyes the "size of dinner plates."

The witness also said, "At intervals of about every eight feet from its head to its tail a substance that had the appearance of a copper band encircled its body, and it was from these many bands that the powerful electric current appeared to come."

The bizarre creature also had two horn-like protrusions sticking from its head. Since the beast was caterpillar-like, perhaps they were antennae? Even stranger, these two "horns" were spraying water that looked like "blue fire" because of its electric charge.

The newspaper account said, "The monster slowly drew in toward the shore, and as it approached from its head poured out a stream of water that looked like blue fire. All the while the air seemed to be filled with electricity, and the sensation experienced was as if each man had on a suit of clothes formed of the fine points of needles. One of the men from the surveyor's camp incautiously took a few steps in the direction of the water, and as he did so the monster darted towards the shore and threw a stream of water that reached the man, and he instantly fell to the ground and lay as though dead."

A second man, Mr. McDonald, rushed to help the fallen surveyor, but he too was struck by the water and fell to the ground. "Mr. McDonald attempted to reach the man's body to pull it back to a place of safety, but he was struck with some of the water that the monster was throwing and fell senseless to the earth. By this time every man in both parties was panic-stricken, and we rushed to the woods for a place of safety, leaving the fallen men lying on the beach."

Even from inside the protection of the trees, the men said they could see the monster's glow light up the sky, and its thunderous roar could be heard for miles around. Luckily for them, the monster never came ashore and instead changed course diving underneath the water. Although it was no longer on the surface, the men could still see the monster's glow as it traveled under the water. Eventually, its glow faded away, and the monster was never seen again.

The men made their way back to their fallen companions. Luckily, the two men were not dead, just knocked unconscious by the mysterious water.

OLD WEST UFOS: 1865-1895

When asked for a detailed description of the monster, one of the witnesses said, "This monster fish, or whatever you may call it, was fully 150 feet long, and at its thickest part I should judge about thirty feet in circumference. Its shape was somewhat out of the ordinary in so far that the body was neither round nor flat but oval, and from what we could see the upper part of the body was covered with a very coarse hair.

"The head was shaped very much like the head of a walrus, though, of course, very much larger. Its eyes, of which it apparently had six, were as large around as a dinner plate, and were exceedingly dull, and it was about the only spot on the monster that at one time or another was not illuminated.

"At intervals of about every eight feet from its head to its tail a substance that had the appearance of a copper band encircled its body and it was from these many bands that the powerful electric current appeared to come. The bands nearest the head seemed to have the strongest electric force, and it was from the first six bands that the most brilliant lights were emitted.

"Near the center of its head were two large horn-like substances, though they could not have been horns, for it was through them that the electrically charged water was thrown.

"Its tail from what I could see of it was shaped like a propeller, and seemed to revolve, and it may be possible that the strange monster pushes himself through the water by means of this propeller like tail."

AN ELECTRIC MONSTER

Flashes of Light and Terrible Sounds Emitted by One in the Bay.

W. L. McDonald Struck Senseless in Attempting to Rescue a Shocked Comrade.

Nearly 150 Feet Long and Covered With Coarse Hair—A Fishing Party's Trip Cut Short.

A party of Tacoma gentlemen have good reason to remember the morning of the 2d of July as long as life remains in their bodies—and to quote the exact words of one of the party, "There are denizens of the ocean that man never, in his most horrible and fantastic nightmare, even saw the likes of."

On Saturday morning a party, composed of the following well known gentlemen, set sail on the sloop "Marion" from the boat house at the end of the wharf for a three days' fishing and hunting excursion on the Sound. The party consisted of Auctioneer William Fitzhenry, H. L. Beal, W. L. McDonald, J. K. Bell, Henry Blackwood and two eastern gentlemen who are visiting the coast, and it is from the lips of one of these gentlemen, who declines to allow his name to be used, as he says that shortly before he left the east he took the Keeley cure, and he fears that if his name was used in connection with this article his eastern friends might think he had "gone back" and got 'em again.

The party were well supplied with all the necessaries of life, as well as an abundance of its luxuries, though it must not be inferred from this fact that the luxuries played any part in creating the sights seen on that memorable morning. Of course, as a person having much respect for truth, I merely chronicle the story as told me, and leave each reader of this remarkable yarn to judge for themselves the necessary amount of credence to give it.

Excerpt from the article about the incident that appeared in the Tacoma (Washington) News Ledger from July 3, 1893.

While this mysterious apparition may seem more like a sea monster than an unidentified object, the "creature" seemed more machine than flesh and blood. As is the case with many Old West UFO sightings, the objects were often described using the characteristics of known animals, such as birds, fish, and insects. In this case, the strange object seemed to be in the shape of an animal, but it may well have been a mechanical device.

In support of the machine theory, witnesses said the monster's body was encircled by something that looked like copper wire. The witnesses also said the monster's tail was like the propeller, spinning round and round. Also, the six eyes as large as dinner plates could easily have been portholes, allowing the ship's occupants to see outside their vessel.

1869 Drawing of Jules Verne's Nautilus (Wikipedia)

This amazing story was published in the *Tacoma Daily Ledger*, on July 3, 1893. It appears to have been based mainly on the testimony of one of the fishermen, whose name was not given. He was not identified, except to say that he was "from the East."

In the last mention of this mysterious eyewitness, the man told the newspaper, "I am going to send a full account of our encounter to the Smithsonian institute, and I doubt not but what they will send out some scientific chaps to investigate. Now I must be going, as I have to leave on tonight's train, but if you need any further particulars you can obtain them from any of the party. No, I do not know who composed the survey party; all I know about them is that they are from Olympia and that they were on the island running farm lines on some disputed land."

Although it remains a very intriguing account from the Old West, critics say that perhaps the witness made up the story for the amusement of their friends. Or if not the witness, then perhaps the reporter himself. Maddeningly for researchers, this was indeed an era rife with yellow journalism. Many stories had a habit of ending just like this one too, with the witness vowing to take proof of their encounter to the Smithsonian.

Interestingly, the famous Jules Verne novel, *Twenty Thousand Leagues under the Sea*, was published in French in 1869 and in English in 1873. The novel is about an eccentric inventor who builds the world's first submarine. To the sailors who see it, the vessel appears to be a huge sea monster.

So was the Tacoma USO a real mechanical monster, or was it a hoax that should have never been published as a true news story? Regardless of whether it is true or not, the story remains the 19th century's most fascinating account of an underwater submersible object.

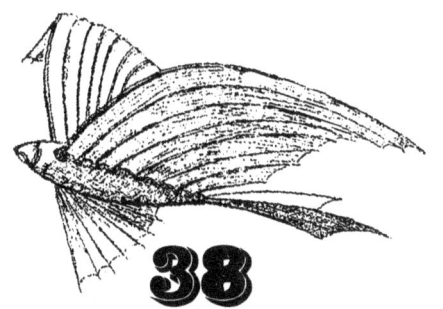

INVASION OF THE FLYING SAUCERS
1893
Kirksville & Leslie, Kentucky

OVER THE YEARS, the state of Kentucky has had a unique history in Ufology, having been the site of several important, well-known UFO encounters, not the least of which was the 1955 case of the "Hopkinsville Goblins." But it was two fascinating 1893 Kentucky UFO encounters about 100 miles apart that we will examine in this chapter – two UFO cases that may very well have been the state's first.

The first case begins with a sleigh ride on a bitterly cold night. On the evening of Monday, January 16, 1893, William O'Connor, 19, of Kirksville was in a sleigh drawn by "two fleet horses," traversing a snowy landscape headed to a party at Kirksville. With him in the sleigh were two

THE REAL COWBOYS & ALIENS

young men and two young women, whose names were not disclosed.

Typical Horse-Drawn Sleigh, Circa 1905

According to an account in the February 6, 1893 edition of the *Marion [Ohio] Daily Star*: "The night was cold, and a light snow was falling, but it was not too dark to see objects twenty-five yards away."

Reaching a point about three miles southwest of Kirksville, one of the men saw a "brilliant light" over on a hillside, about 100 yards from the roadside, and he called the attention of the others to it.

The witnesses at first thought it was the reflection of a lamp burning in a house nearby, but that theory was nixed as the glow of the light was far brighter than anything that could come from a lamp. O'Connor later described the light as "electric in brilliancy," and stressed that no persons were anywhere near the light source, because if there had been, the brightness of the light would have disclosed them.

As the young men and women watched the dazzling light, they saw it begin to rise off the ground, while also slowly spinning around in a circle, until it was high up from the ground. After a while, the strange object again came back down to the ground while making "large circles."

Their curiosity extremely piqued, two of the young men left the safety of their sleigh, waded through deep snowdrifts, and stood in the bitter cold for 15 minutes watching the strange phenomenon from a closer vantage point.

Unable to stand the cold any longer, the men rejoined their companions in the sleigh and resumed their journey to the farmhouse in Kirksville, where the party was scheduled to take place.

To their amazement, the strange light followed them for three miles until they arrived near their destination. Pausing the sleigh at the farm gate leading to the farmhouse, the group saw the spinning light approaching their position and circling around them. They continued watching the strange phenomenon for 15 minutes.

The article unfortunately does not mention how the sighting ended, but it does say that "others ... have witnessed the same sight at or near this spot." The strange motion of the object - traveling up and down and spinning in a circle – seems to eliminate the possibility that the object was a meteor or other heavenly body. In fact, the motion of the object is

THE REAL COWBOYS & ALIENS

probably the reason that the word "meteor" does not appear at all in the newspaper article.

Considering that the object followed the group and then circled around it, one must wonder if the group narrowly avoided being abducted. Perhaps it was the presence of other people at the nearby farmhouse that saved them.

In conclusion, our research finds that William O' Connor was an actual person who lived in the Kirksville area during this time. Born in 1873, he lists his occupation as "day laborer" in the 1900 U.S. Census.

Later that same year, in late summer, about 100 miles southwest of Kirksville, there was an even more perplexing UFO sighting where many of the residents of tiny Leslie, Kentucky, observed a multitude of flying discs. The event was so unbelievable that they thought Judgment Day was upon them. Although thought to be, at the time, some kind of "solar phenomenon," this incident has all the earmarks of an actual UFO encounter. The article, appropriately titled "Judgment Day," first appeared in the August 20, 1893 edition of the *St. Louis (Missouri) Globe-Democrat.*

On August 19, residents of the tiny hamlet near Burkesville, Kentucky, were waking up and preparing to begin another day. About 30 minutes after sunrise, people noticed a sudden change in the appearance of the sun, which turned "a very peculiar color."

Shielding their eyes with their hands and turning to look toward the sun, the residents saw "thousands of disks, seemingly about the size of a wagon wheel," which filled the entire sky. Each individual disk was observed to be "in motion." Their colors varied from bright red to green to black, as well as other colors.

> **GHOSTLY LIGHTS**
>
> **Sensational Experience of a Kentucky Sleighing Party.**
>
> RICHMOND, Ky., Feb. 6.—William O'Connor, who resides at Kirksville, in this county, is very much puzzled and excited over an experience he had with a ghastly fire phenomenon, three miles from this city, recently. He professes to be a skeptic on the subject of spiritualism, and relates a remarkable and interesting story of his late adventure.
>
> In company with two young men and two young ladies, Mr. O'Connor left Richmond, on Monday night, Jan. 16, in a sleigh drawn by two fleet horses. They were on thier way to a party at Kirksville.
>
> The night was cold, and a light snow was falling, but it was not too dark to see objects twenty-five yards away. When they reached a point about three miles southwest of this city one of the young men saw a brilliant light over on a hillside, about one hundred yards from the roadside, and called attention to the party to it.
>
> The crowd thought it was the reflection of a lamp burning in a house nearby, but as the latter was 300 yards away and the light on the hillside exceedingly bright, they were unwilling to accept this. They stopped to investigate the strange scene. At this time the light began to slowly circle round, rising a great distance from the ground, then falling to the earth again in large circles.
>
> Mr. O'Connor describes the appearance of the light as electric in brilliancy, and says there was no human near the spot; had there been he would have been visible, as the light was so bright. The curiosity of the young men arose to a high pitch at this time, and two of them alighted and waded through deep snowdrifts, and stood for a quarter of an hour watching the strange phenomenon.
>
> Being chilled, the party resumed their journey. They drove to the farmhouse where the party was to be given, and witnessed the same peculiar spectacle which they had come in contact with an hour before. At the farm gate they again watched the light another quarter of an hour, which continued to approach them, circling as it came.
>
> Mr. O'Connor and companions are unable to fathom the mystery, and others who have witnessed the same sight at or near this spot are likewise puzzled to know what it is.

The Marion (Ohio) Star, 2-6-1893, p.1

Based on the witnesses, the spinning disks were descending from the sky toward the ground, and interestingly, as they approached the ground, their shape would change from disk-shaped to triangular or square or other shapes. Also, as they approached, the colors of all disks changed to a dense purple color.

According to the witnesses "the sun would swallow-up some of the disks, and then again they would appear to sink into the solid ground and then disappear." Apparently no sound accompanied these discs, for "There was no noise save that made by the mountain folks, who, whenever a disk would come directly at them, would either run away at a great rate or fall to their knees and pray."

The article concludes by stating, "The phenomenon lasted fully an hour, and when it was over the natives were pleased, for they were positive that judgment day had come, and they were not prepared therefor."

> **JUDGMENT DAY.**
>
> A Solar Phenomenon Startles the People of Cumberland County, Ky.
>
> Special Dispatch to the Globe-Democrat.
>
> CINCINNATI, O., August 19.—The residents of Leslie, a small hamlet in Cumberland County, near Burksville, Ky., were in a terrible state of excitement yesterday morning from a most unaccountable freak of the sun, or its rays. About half an hour after the rising of the sun the country people around the little village were thrown into a state of consternation that bordered on the ludicrous, had it no been for the intense fear the simple folks entertained. They thought that "judgment day" had come. Many of the best people of this section can not explain the phenomenon, and it has no parallel in the memory of the oldest inhabitant. The facts, as well as could be gathered by the GLOBE-DEMOCRAT correspondent, were about as follows: When the sun was up only a few moments it was observed to be of a very peculiar color. The attention of several people was called to it, and while they were looking at it thousands of disks, seemingly about the size of a wagon wheel, were seen to fill the entire heavens, and all of them seemed to be in motion and to fill the heavens from the earth to the sun. The bodies were described as being round in shape until they approached the earth, when they would change to different shapes, some becoming triangular, some square and others taking on various proportions and odd forms. The colors of the disks were also said to be of different shades—some bright red, some green, black, etc., but when they reached the earth all assumed a dense purple color. It appeared to those witnessing the phenomenon that the sun would swallow up some of the disks, and then again they would appear to sink into the solid grounds and then reappear. There was no noise save that made by the mountain folks, who, whenever a disk would come directly at them, would either run away at a great rate or fall on their knees and pray. The phenomenon lasted fully an hour, and when it was over the natives were pleased, for they were positive that judgment day had come, and they were not prepared therefor.
>
> St. Louis (Missouri) Globe-Democrat, 8-20-1893, p. 9

The newspaper writer noted that nobody could remember an event of this nature ever before, and it certainly does not seem to have been any kind of natural solar occurrence. UFO researchers over the years have concluded that this must have been a true encounter with some type of incredibly sophisticated craft.

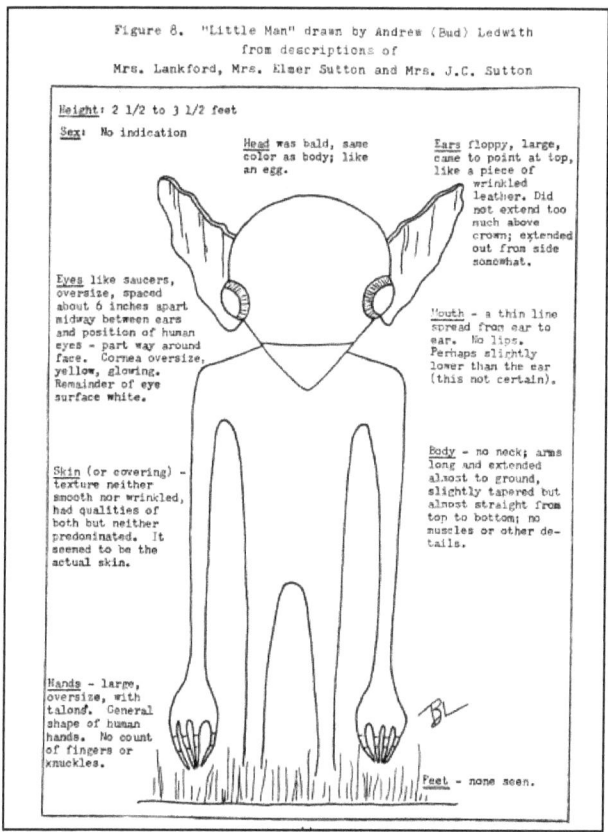

One of the "Hopkinsville Goblins"

In more recent years, Kentucky has had some of the oddest UFO encounters of all time, including an incident on August 21, 1955, when a group of literal "Little Green Men" besieged a farmhouse near Hopkinsville, Kentucky. That night, a large family of five adults and seven children arrived at the local police station stating exasperatedly that they had been warding off alien invaders with a shotgun for the past two hours! Police returned to the home to investigate, finding no trace of the aliens, but seeing plenty of damage from the shotgun blasts.

The story became a newspaper sensation, and the aliens, called the "Hopkinsville Goblins," were described as having "large pointed ears, claw-like hands, eyes that glowed yellow and spindly legs." Perhaps it was these same strange beings that were also behind the UFO sightings of 1893? We will probably never know....

INDEX

A Princess of Mars, 16
Adamstown, Pennsylvania, 35
alien beings
   as "little people", 160
   as "Reptilian", 47, 277-283
   as "water babies", 41-48
   as giants, 185
   as humanoid, 82
   as Martians, 18
alien hieroglyphics, 19, 188-189
Apache Indians, 179
Area 51, 41-42
Aurora, Texas, 10
ball lightning, 71-73
Benkelman, Nebraska, 191, 197
Bigfoot, 215-220, 253-254
Billy the Kid, 8
Bloomington, Indiana, 87
Bonham, Texas, 59
Brazel, Jesse Wayne, 10
Brazel, Mack, 10
Brorsen's Comet, 135, 139
Brownsville, Missouri, 74-78
Burroughs, Edgar Rice, 16
Cameron Mills, New York, 159
Chisum, John, 8-9
Civil War, 7, 173
Clark, Jerome, 271
Costa, Cheryl, 138-139, 159, 162
Crawfordsville, Indiana, 144, 268
Dallas, Texas, 93-95, 237
Denton, Professor William, 13-20
Dublin, Texas, 261-265
Dubuque, Iowa, 145
Earp, Wyatt, 9
Edwards, Frank, 232
Edwardsville, Kansas, 121
Fate magazine, 167
First Transcontinental Railroad, 8
Fort Scott, Kansas, 58-60
Fort, Charles, 201, 267
Galisteo, New Mexico, 151-157
Garrett, Pat, 9
Gettysburg, Pennsylvania, 173
Hall, Mark A., 251
Hickok, "Wild Bill", 7
Hickson, Charles, 65
Holiday, Doc, 9
Hopkins, Dr. Herbert, 50
Hopkinsville Goblins, 293, 299
Hopkinsville, Kentucky, 298
Hynek, Dr. J. Allen, 95-96
Indio, California, 103
James, Jesse, 7
Jessup, Morris K., 139

Jupiter, 129-134, 274
Keyhoe, Donald, 60
Kirksville, Kentucky, 293-296
Kirkwood, Professor Daniel, 89
Lincoln County War, 8-9
Lizard Man, 282
Lockyer, J. Norman, 113-119
Long Lake, Connecticut, 221-222
Lordsburg, New Mexico, 9, 251
Louisville, Kentucky, 165
Madisonville, Kentucky, 170
Marfa Lights, 175-183
Mars, 10, 13, 16-20, 37, 185, 188
McKeesport, Pennsylvania, 133
Men in Black, 10, 49, 50, 51, 53, 55, 190
Nampa, Idaho, 227, 229
Norwood, New York, 201
Paiute Indians, 44-48
Paris, Texas, 237, 243
Parker, Calvin, 66, 69
Pascagoula UFO Incident of 1973, 65
Pascagoula, Mississippi, 65-72
Pathfinder (hot air balloon), 145-149
Presidio, Texas, 180
Putnam, Professor Frederic Ward, 230-231

Pyramid Lake, Nevada, 41-48, 227
Roswell Incident, The, 10, 19, 151, 157, 189, 191
Roswell, New Mexico, 9, 151, 156, 191
San Antonio, Texas, 180
Scape Ore Swamp, South Carolina, 281
Scientific American, 87, 90, 141, 227, 231-232
Sheridan, Pennsylvania, 81
Southern Pacific Railway, 178
Spring-Heeled Jack, 166-173
Steiger, Brad, 14-15, 20, 219
Swift, Dr. Lewis, 208
Tacoma, Washington, 221, 284
Taylorsville, Ohio, 51
Tombstone, Arizona, 8, 245, 251
unidentified flying object
   as airship, 107, 109, 145-146, 149, 151-152, 155-156, 192, 197, 237-238, 241-243
   as drones, 37, 76, 97
   as flying disk, 93
   as ghost ship, 103-107
   as living creature, 9, 57, 245, 267
   as luminous object, 35, 68

as orbs of light, 52, 73, 294
  as part of a fleet, 87
  as phantom train, 121-122
unidentified submersible object, 221, 284

Union Pacific Railway, 115
Venus, 16, 132-133, 207
Virginia City, Nevada, 8
Wise, John, 143, 144, 145
Yuma, Arizona, 104

ABOUT THE AUTHOR

Noe Torres is a recognized expert in the field of UFOs and the paranormal. He is an author, publisher, and member of the Mutual UFO Network (MUFON). He holds a Bachelor's in English and a Master's in Library Science from the University of Texas at Austin. He has written one of the most popular books about the famous Roswell Incident, titled *Ultimate Guide to the Roswell UFO Crash*, which is the top selling book among tourists visiting Roswell, New Mexico. He has also written several other well-reviewed books, including *Mexico's Roswell*, *The Other Roswell*, *Aliens in the Forest*, *Fallen Angel*, and *The Coyame Incident*.

Noe has appeared on several nationally-broadcast television shows, including season 2, episode 1 of the Travel Channel's *Mysteries of the Outdoors*, titled "Strange Attraction," which premiered in August 2017. In that show, he is interviewed extensively about unexplained mysteries in Big Bend National Park. Also, in 2017, Noe was featured in an episode titled "The Marfa Lights" for the TV series *Mysteries of the Unexplained*. In 2008, he appeared in season 1, episode 4 of the

History Channel's *UFO Hunters*, in a show called "Crash and Retrieval."

Noe has appeared several times on George Noory's famous radio show *Coast to Coast AM*, as well as on The Jeff Rense Program and may other shows. He is also in high demand as a speaker at UFO and paranormal conferences and festivals, having been a featured speaker at the 2017 International UFO Congress in Scottsdale, Arizona. He has also spoken five times at the annual Roswell UFO Conference and at many other UFO conferences throughout the United States and Mexico.

ABOUT THE AUTHOR

John LeMay was born and raised in Roswell, NM, the "UFO Capital of the World." He is the author of over twenty books on film and western history such as *Kong Unmade: The Lost Films of Skull Island*, *Tall Tales and Half Truths of Billy the Kid*, and *Roswell USA: Towns That Celebrate UFOs, Lake Monsters, Bigfoot and Other Weirdness*. He has written for magazines such as *True West*, *Cinema Retro*, and *Mad Scientist* and is himself the editor/publisher of *The Lost Films Fanzine*. He is a Past President of the Board of Directors for the Historical Society for Southeast New Mexico.

ALSO AVAILABLE

COMING SOON

ALSO AVAILABLE

ALSO AVAILABLE

www.ingramcontent.com/pod-product-compliance
Lightning Source LLC
Chambersburg PA
CBHW071334080526
44587CB00017B/2830